I GOT TO LIVE WITH

an Angel

The Story of a Remarkable Woman and her Journey with Brain Cancer

I GOT TO LIVE WITH
an Angel

JEFFREY D. NELSON, M.D.

First Edition

ISBN: 9781946195890
LOC: 2021903385

First Printing March 2021
Cover and Interior design by FuzionPress

FuzionPress
1250 E 115th Street
Burnsville, MN 55337
612-781-2815

To bulk order copies, please contact the author via jnelson9215@comcast.net

TABLE OF CONTENTS

Chapter One

BEGINNING OF A JOURNEY

It was a day like any other day. I had gotten up in the morning, showered, eaten my breakfast, read the newspaper, given my wife Jane a kiss and headed off to work at the clinic. I am a family physician and have worked for the same clinic since 1982 in a town called Cottage Grove, Minnesota. Jane and I moved here after I finished my residency at St. Paul Ramsey Hospital in St. Paul, Minnesota. We raised our three children here.

But then I was sitting at my desk at the clinic when Jane paged me at 7:41 a.m. She said her mom had called to say she had some vaginal bleeding, was concerned, and was going to go to the doctor. Jane was thinking about whether she should go with to help keep track of things. Her mom had some memory problems and would be 86 years old in ten days. Also, her mom had had placenta previa when she was pregnant with her brother David many years ago and had bled severely at the time of his delivery. She would appropriately be anxious that this bleeding could be something serious. But Jane and I both decided that she did not have to go over to be with her mom right at that moment. Her dad would take her mom to the appointment. Then we would see what we needed to do to be helpful for them. I started seeing my first patients and quickly forgot about this given the busyness of the morning.

Jane paged me again just after 9 a.m. and said something to the effect that she had hurt her shoulder and that Carol (Woodward) was with her. I do not remember exactly what she said as I am writing this on April 6, 2014. What a journey it has been since that Tuesday the 4th of March.

Jane paged me again about half an hour later. It was not like her to be paging me unless something significant was happening. I remember she was repeating things she had told me earlier. When I said something about this, she was telling me to just listen to her.

I later learned that Carol had called her a little after 8 o'clock and they were going to go walking together as usual. When Carol then came to the house to get Jane to walk, there was no answer. Since that was unexpected, Carol went to our neighbors, the Bexell's, and phoned Jane from there. Jane answered the phone but did not sound right. Jane gave her the garage code so she could get in the house. She came over and found Jane on our bed, just sitting there. Her shoulder was very sore, so they put it in a sling. They felt she was doing ok and that I did not need to come immediately.

I called when I was done with morning patients at the clinic and Jane said she could not get out of bed because her feet were too sore. Even though it had been a crazy morning at the clinic, and I knew the afternoon was going to be terribly busy, I knew I just had to go home and see what was going on. When I got home and examined her, she was in bed, alert and talking clearly. But when I put pressure on her left upper arm, that immediately hurt so it looked like she had a fracture. Her feet had a little bruising but did not look bad, but she said they were too sore to walk on. Her tongue was also sore. There was a small spot of blood on the carpet at the foot of the bed. She had an abrasion on her left knee, and I thought that was probably the source of the blood on the carpet, but later realized that with the long pants she had on and the fact they were not torn, it did not make sense that was the source of the blood. (Later when our daughter Sarah cleaned up the carpet, she noticed some saliva like material with the blood.)

I checked the clinic schedule and asked one of my partners if she could see Jane to check things out. Jane's usual physician, Julie Vogel, was not in that day. The left humerus x-ray did show a subcapital humeral fracture. Her EKG was normal. Jane had had episodes of syncope before, when there was some type of pain, like an ankle sprain, that caused a vasovagal syncope or fainting episode. We wanted to believe that this episode was caused by that even though there was nothing that we knew of that would have caused her pain that morning before the episode. I later thought I should have just had her call the paramedics or taken her to the ER when I came home at noon, but it did not seem necessary at the time.

We did not realize it then, but Jane had had her first seizure. As a family physician, I should have immediately thought of that as a possibility, but why would my healthy wife who just celebrated her 60th birthday in December have a seizure? If Jane had been driving to her mom's place when the first seizure occurred, she could have easily been killed in the accident. If she had not had the intuition to carry the phone with her upstairs where that first seizure occurred, she could have been there much longer before being found. If she and Carol had not been planning on walking together, it could also have been much longer.

Another challenge had begun, but also the miracles and blessings.

There is so much that I want to tell you, but it takes time to tell the full story of any life.

A friend of ours- Cheryl Bostrom- wrote the following note to Jane not long after her diagnosis.

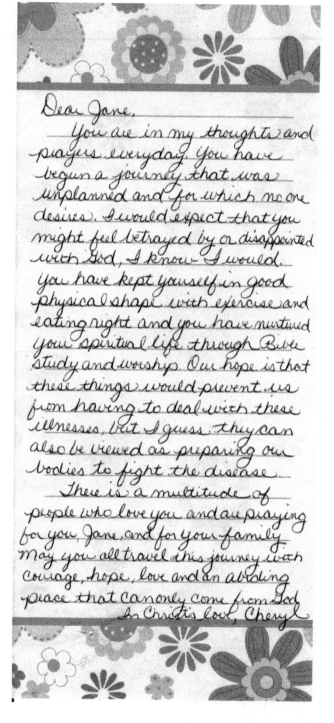

Dear Jane,

You are in my thoughts and prayers everyday. You have begun a journey that was unplanned and for which no one desires. I would expect that you might feel betrayed by or disappointed with God, I know I would. You have kept yourself in good physical shape with exercise and eating right and you have nurtured your spiritual life through Bible study and worship. Our hope is that these things would prevent us from having to deal with these illnesses, but I guess they can also be viewed as preparing our bodies to fight the disease.

There is a multitude of people who love you and are praying for you, Jane, and for your family. May you all travel this journey with courage, hope, love and an abiding peace that can only come from God.

In Christ's love, Cheryl

Jeffrey D. Nelson M.D. ♦ 10

Chapter Two

MEETING JANE

Jane and I both started attending Luther College in Decorah, Iowa in the fall of 1972. She had graduated from high school in Burnsville, Minnesota. I grew up in Camanche, Iowa. Burnsville had a graduating class with over 500 students. My class was just shy of 90. On March 2, 1973 (according to a letter that Jane had sent to her friend Jody on March 8th) (I had always thought it was late January or early February) there was a "freshman mixer "- a dance to give students a chance to meet each other. I was in a Larson Hall dorm room and my roommate was Steve Schick- from Mason City, Iowa. Jane was in Brandt Hall and had two roommates- Sara Gaylor and Kathy Ehredt. The mixer was in their dorm. I had tried asking several girls to go out in the fall of 1972 at Luther, but nothing really lasted or seemed significant. I had tried dating a number of girls in high school, but always felt awkward. I wonder if God knew that He had the right partner for me. I do not believe that God plans everything out, but who knows.

That night at the mixer, I saw a girl with beautiful blonde hair, blue eyes with such a twinkle, a smile that told you the meaning of joy, wearing long white pants and a blue blouse. She and her roommate Kathy came over to talk with the group of guys that I had come with from our dorm. I got up the courage to ask her to dance and she accepted. What a joy to hold her hand as we danced! But when the dance was done, she immediately started walking away. I followed her because I think I knew even then that I was falling in love with her. She was not walking away because she disliked me, she was just shy. We danced several more times, some of the songs were "slow" where you could hold each other closer. How wonderful that was!

This was the way that Jane described it in her letter to Jody:

"Last Friday night we had a Freshman mixer in our lounge. There was a group of guys just sitting around so Kathy and I went to talk to them. Then this one guy asked me to dance. We danced about 5 times- 3 slow ones [mmmmmm] then we went to my room and talked with Kathy and some other guys that dropped in {til 1:00 a.m.}. We had such a good time. I was hoping he would call Saturday but nothing.......... (as usual). Then Sunday afternoon he called and asked if I wanted to go to a Jazz concert in Dantes. After that we talked in the lounge. Then Monday night he called and said that he could not study and was wondering if I wanted to come over and listen to records. That was at 6:30. At 11:00 we went for a walk along the river. It sounded so neat cuz everything is thawing. I did not hear anything on Tuesday but last night he called and asked if I wanted to go to a movie Friday night (Alice's Restaurant). Honestly, I've been to so many movies lately. This is sort of a sketchy view, but I'll tell you more later...................Never felt this way before!"

I had never felt that way before either. We found we could talk about anything. Over the next several months, we spent more time together, often studying at the library near each other. We both knew that doing well at school was important for our future and often were at the library till near closing time.

But we also had fun. As it warmed up, one day we went to Malanaphy Springs outside Decorah. After a Midwest winter and the coldness, it is so wonderful to experience the spring- the sunshine, the warm weather, the breezes. It just lifts your spirit after having to deal with the winter coldness. We had so much fun just being together.

We were nearing finals which were usually in mid-May. On my birthday, I learned more about how special Jane was. Neither one of us had any money- we were both stretching the few dollars that we had till we got back to our summer jobs. I did not expect her to get me any birthday present, certainly nothing of significance. That birthday turned out to be one of the most special I have ever experienced. She had made me several presents- each one wrapped, each one special in some way. She had observed my comments, and my behaviors and tailored each small present to be something that I would appreciate. The fact that she did this with almost no financial resources was even more special. But the most wonderful present was the smile on her face, the hug she gave me, the way that she showed that she cared about me. How can a guy not feel on cloud 9 when the first girl that he ever really got excited about treats him this way!

Finishing the semester at Luther and having to go home to work for the summer and be apart from Jane was difficult. This was also a prelude to realizing how often Jane was considering how someone else felt. She would remember a comment by someone that would tell her what the best gift was for that person at Christmas or know how to make a comment to include them in the conversation if that was difficult for them.... She just knew how to show others that she cared about them. She knew that each one of us is special.

When it came time to leave Luther that spring and go back home, I did not really want to do that. In 1973, there were no cell phones or instant messaging or Twitter or Facebook. Long distance phone calls were expensive and not part of your phone plan, so Jane and I wrote many letters to each other that summer. At that time first class postage was 8 cents. Having to be apart only grew us closer together. I so looked forward to returning to Luther that fall.

Chapter Three

SEIZURE!

We both were uncomfortable that we did not better understand why she had that episode on Tuesday morning. I was able to get her an appointment to see her usual family physician, Dr. Vogel on Friday, March 7th. After seeing her, she was scheduled for an MRI of her brain that night, a neurology appointment for March 19th, and a Holter monitor at Woodwinds Hospital outpatient cardiology department on the 14th.

We got some supper. Later that evening we headed to Woodwinds Hospital to have the outpatient MRI of the brain. It took a little over an hour and we headed back home. We were concerned, hoping it was not going to show anything serious. We were both getting used to sleeping in bed in such a way that we did not cause her left arm to move which would increase her pain. If she held still, she would have little pain and she managed with just Tylenol. But if she moved the shoulder the wrong way, irritating the fracture site, it was extremely painful.

The following morning, we both woke early. We went down to get breakfast, and we were sitting at the breakfast table having our usual cereal and juice. It was not long when suddenly, Jane stood up. But then I realized her face was grimacing and she quickly went into a full body convulsion! If I had not been able to stand up quickly and catch her, she would have fallen flat to the floor, further injuring her left arm and body. She was in a full generalized tonic-clonic seizure. I laid her on her right side as gently as I could so that she would not hurt her left shoulder. At first, I did not know what else to do, but as the seizure continued, I got the phone and called 911.

As a family physician, I had learned about basic seizure management in medical school and residency, but it is entirely different when it is your loved one- your wife- who has been entirely healthy, and you are certainly not expecting this to happen.

It seemed like forever before the paramedics arrived, but I know it was less than 10 minutes from when I called. Fortunately, the new police station was less than a mile from our house and it was a short trip for them. I had unlocked the door for them to be able to come in. Otherwise, I had stayed at Jane's side. The convulsion had started to subside before they arrived. But Jane was groggy, slowly starting to come out of it.

The paramedics had to ask all the basic questions, her name, birthdate, medications she was on, what happened, etc. They helped her get on the gurney and took her out to the paramedic van to place an IV in her arm before leaving for the hospital. She had veins that were always difficult to put IVs in. It usually required more than one stick before someone could place an IV in Jane, even if they were very experienced.

She had had multiple surgeries in her lifetime already. As many others have, she had her wisdom teeth removed as a teenager. In the process of being evaluated for that surgery, she had a chest x-ray that showed a mass by her spine. There were no CAT scans or MRIs at that time. That meant she had to have a thoracotomy to surgically remove the mass. It turned out to be a benign tumor that was near her spinal cord. She healed well from that, the only residual being the large scar under her left arm.

Our first son, Chris, was in the breech position, so Jane had to have a Caesarean section for his delivery. She had two further C sections for our other children Tom and Sarah. She had had a bladder surgery in the 1990s for urethral pseudopolyps that were due to multiple urinary tract infections. But for all these events, she was a healthy 60-year-old woman starting the year of 2014.

The paramedics drove her to the Woodwinds Emergency room, and I followed in our red 2007 Honda CRV. It all seemed so unreal.

When we got to the ER, they hooked Jane up to the EKG, drew blood, and the physician talked with the radiologist when he learned she had had an MRI of the brain just the night before. We found out that the MRI indeed showed a mass in the right parietal area of her brain that was about 1 inch in diameter. Apparently, the tech working the night before had thought that there was something there but had not asked the on-call radiologist to look at it before we left the hospital. Since then, I understand that the hospital and radiology group changed the protocol to have the radiologist review the scan before the patient leaves.

But there is no perfect way to handle these situations. Not all radiologists are the best skilled at reading brain scans, and so they have the neuroradiologists read these scans. One cannot expect a neuroradiologist to be available 24/7 at every facility that does scans and read them before the patient leaves the facility.

Not long after we arrived at the emergency room, I called Gary Valencour, a good friend of ours from church. Gary was a part of a men's group that I would get together with most Saturday mornings. His wife Ellie was a close friend of Jane's. They came to the hospital to support us within the hour. The ER physician contacted the neurologist on call- Dr. Marcel Hungs. He had them start IV Keppra(levetiracetam) to try to prevent further seizures and told them to admit her for further workup.

The hospitalist who cared for Jane was Matt Rolando. I had worked with him over the years. I knew he was very competent and that made me feel more comfortable. It was only about 5 years ago that hospitalists had become the standard for primary care in the hospital. Before that, our family physicians and internists that worked at the various clinics in the area also saw all the patients from their group in the hospital when that care was needed. There is no perfect way to organize medical care. There are pros and cons to every option that exists.

Over the course of that Saturday, Jane had CT scans of her chest, abdomen, pelvis, and neck area and every scan came back normal. A neurosurgery consult was ordered. Dr. Richard Gregory came to Woodwinds on Sunday afternoon to talk with and examine Jane and reviewed the head MRI scan with us. We hoped that this could be an infection that could be treated, or a very treatable cancer like a lymphoma, but as Dr. Gregory said, the only way to know was to have surgery to biopsy and remove the abnormal tissue. I knew that Jane had to have surgery, but I was afraid of the possible complications. Dr. Gregory was reassuring but also straightforward in discussing the risks and benefits of the surgery. He said that if we wanted to worry, we should worry about the possibility of a stroke related to bleeding from blood vessels in the field of the surgery.

Jane had been stable since admission on Saturday morning and the necessary workup had been done. She wanted to return home, and she was able to be discharged early on the evening of Sunday, March 9th. Despite a busy neurosurgery schedule, Dr. Gregory was able to schedule Jane for her craniotomy on Wednesday, March 12th.

On March 11th, Jane sent an email to Rolf and Nancy Olson that she was having surgery the next day and to let them know some of the events of the last week. Rolf and Nancy had been friends of ours since we had met when each of us had a child in the same high school musical play-Godspell. She asked them to keep us in their prayers. She ended up asking others to be on her prayer team. Her team also included Ellie Valencour, Mary Beard, Linda Stoner, Irene Detviler, Ronda Keller, Dennis & Cheryl Bostrom, all friends of ours from church, my stepmother Elinor Nelson, my sister Nancy Kedley, as well as Lori Burkhart and Dan & Sherrie Vos who were friends of ours from my medical school days.

Chapter Four

PATIENCE IS A VIRTUE

Jane had had patience waiting for me to come home so many times over the years. When I was in residency, we commonly were on call every third night staying in the hospital overnight to care for the patients, and then still working a full day the next day. You never knew when you were going to get done. When I had been up most of the night, and then worked all day, I would be exhausted. When I was able to get home, Jane would have supper for me. More than once, I fell asleep at the supper table. She would have been ready for some companionship and my body was telling me to sleep. Out of the cycle of three days, Jane and I would only have a short time on the evening of the third day that we could actually talk with one another. That time when I was a family medicine resident was the most difficult on our relationship simply because of the lack of time that we could spend together, and the fact that I was often exhausted when we were together.

She had to have patience on the day of her first neurosurgery on March 12, 2014 when she had to wait 11 hours from the time she got to the hospital until they took her back to the operating room. We had to be there at 5 a.m. and the nurse who admitted her did the basic vital signs and review of history. She had to have both a CT of her brain as well as an MRI. The neurosurgery team placed fiducials on her scalp so that when she was put in the stereotactic machine the surgeon would know exactly where to make the incision and go for the mass in her brain. After that she was back in the pre-surgery holding room. An anesthesiologist came in around 9 a.m. to put in an arterial line in her right wrist. This is done to monitor blood pressure closely during some surgeries. Her surgery was scheduled for about 11 a.m. Chris, Tom and Sarah were all present as we waited for her to be taken back to the operating room. The minutes, then hours passed.

In the early afternoon we learned that an emergency cardiac case had taken the team that was to work with Dr. Gregory to do Jane's surgery. There are not extra surgical staff with the right expertise waiting around all day just for you. We knew this, but it still was hard to wait. After waiting all morning and afternoon, Dr. Gregory came in about 5 p.m. and said they would be taking her back soon to the O.R.- almost 12 hours since we had gotten to the hospital that morning.

After surgery, Dr. Gregory talked with the children, their spouses, and me. He told us that it was a type of brain cancer and that it was serious. He showed us some of the MRI scan pictures. It was around 11 p.m. when Jane was transferred from the post-operative recovery room to the neuro ICU. When I saw her, I realized that her arterial line was in her right foot. I found out that the right wrist radial line that had been placed in the morning had clotted and had to be removed. Because of the left arm fracture, the left wrist could not be used. So, they had to place it in the foot, the dorsalis pedis artery. That artery is found in the middle of the top of the arch of the foot. That area would hurt her for some time after the surgery. She had to have a PICC (peripherally inserted central catheter) line placed in her right arm in the ICU around 2 a.m. to get the hypertonic saline that Dr. Gregory ordered. The nurse who did that procedure was very efficient.

After he was done, and Jane was settling down, it was sometime between 3 and 4 a.m. when Jane told me that I was "bugging her". She wanted me to leave and go home to sleep. I had not wanted to leave her side after she came up from neurosurgery. I was afraid with the diagnosis that Dr. Gregory had given us. But I was also exhausted and when she told me that she wanted me to leave, it was a relief.

I drove the 20–25-minute drive to home and got about 2 hours of sleep. When I woke up, I called the ICU to see how she was doing. I came back to the hospital to be with her. I had only been there a short time when she said to me, "I need you to be with me." Between her left arm fracture, the right arm with the PICC line, the right leg with the arterial line, it was about impossible for her to move by herself.

But I had to laugh that only hours earlier she had told me that she wanted me to leave. I think she knew that I needed to get some sleep.

She had to have patience in March of 1980 when Chris was born by C-section and she was not healing like usual. She had gone home after one week in the hospital. After several days at home and in the middle of the night, she told me we needed to go back to the hospital because she felt there was something definitely wrong. She felt like she was going to die. We thought she was distended due to constipation, but it turned out that her bladder had been lacerated when the C-section was done. She had urine draining into her peritoneal cavity and filling it up with fluid, and that was causing her constipation. It also caused essentially kidney failure because the material excreted by the kidneys just recirculated into the body. That was why she felt like she was going crazy. Her exhausted intern husband did not recognize that something terrible was occurring. After the doctor at the hospital (Rob Lund who was in my family medicine residency class) tapped her abdomen and drained the fluid, she felt so much better. She was ready to eat a Big Mac. She had surgery to repair the bladder wall and healed quickly following that.

Chris stayed in the hospital while Jane was there. It is not usual to put a baby back in the hospital just for routine care, but Jane needed to be able to breastfeed him. At first the hospital was going to refuse. We felt it was the least they could do when the cause of her trouble was the surgeon's error. They allowed him to be in the convalescent nursery until Jane was able to be discharged home. Most of her surgery had been done by Gordy Ditmanson who was a fine chief resident in OB and a very caring person. He felt so bad that this happened. But Dr. Eric Hakanson, the staff obstetrician, had initially blamed it on Jane, saying that she had not urinated often enough after the C section, and that that was the cause of the rupture. His behavior could have easily encouraged us to file a lawsuit. What is an intern physician in the program to do? We just wanted Jane to get better.

After I was done with residency and working at the clinic, Family Practitioners, P.A., she had to have patience. Many times, I would be stuck at the clinic and did not get home when I thought I would be home. If it is just one time, that is frustrating but no big deal. Even though I always made it a priority to get home as soon as I got the necessary work done at the clinic, there were frequent times that I was later than expected. It was always so hard to predict when I would be done with the necessary work. Jane would call or page me to get an idea of when to have supper ready. I would try to give an estimate. Then many times, factors that were uncontrollable occurred, and I got home later than I thought.

More than once she told me the story of being in confirmation at Christ the King Lutheran Church in Bloomington as a teenager. Her father would drive her there, and then he would usually be back after confirmation was over. But there were times when he was late, and she would have to wait. Once she waited a long time by herself and was wondering if he was going to show up. In those days, there were no cell phones to contact someone.

Jane learned to have the virtue of patience. In the Bible, according to the book of Galatians 5:25, it is one of the "Fruits of the Spirit".

I recently found a poem in her handwriting that she had written years ago.

Evening

I come home from work, unlock the door, and
Walk into silence. I wonder if you're there.
I look around making sure you aren't
Home yet, wishing that you were.
I make the bed, straighten the magazines,
Open the drapes and wonder.
I see the kids swinging outside and I
wonder who you are caring for, who you are
listening to, I wish it were me.
I turn on the music, pick up my romance
And read, and dream.
Shining knights and beautiful damsels
Loving and sharing and playing. I wonder
When you'll be home.
I turn on the T.V., set the table, sit on
the couch and listen. I wonder when you'll call.
We live, we love, we share, we care.
I wonder.

Chapter Five

LETTERS

Whenever we were not together after we met in March of 1973 and before we married in August 1975, Jane and I wrote letters to each other. As I said earlier, it was a time when long distance calling was more expensive and not something that we could do frequently. So, we wrote letters.

We wrote about what we were doing with our friends, what we did at work, mundane daily things, as well as what amounted to philosophy and life.

On July 28, 1973, Jane had written me a long letter and included the following thoughts-

"There are so many people in this world that want to change what they already are- either in appearance or personality or intelligence-whatever. But one of the things that I think is so great about our relationship is that I love what you are now. I can accept your virtues but most important I can accept your faults too- and believe me we all have many. You may want to change certain things about you but as you go through these changes, I will be willing to accept you. I think that it is important to have someone that will always be there to go to, to love, to receive love from, to talk to and grow to understand. Up to now, my family has been the only source of this security and love. There are _very_ few people who are willing to care for us no matter what we do or how we look, etc. I think that is why a lot of people seek out God- to find this security and hope. You are one of the few people that I truly care for. Partnership is something to value greatly. I have the desire to get to know you better so that I can give to you security, love, someone to go to, someone to talk to.

Thanks for letting me 'talk' to you,
 Love, Jane"

On August 2, 1973, I replied:
Dear Jane,

It was truly great to get your letter Tuesday- a bright spot in an otherwise dreary day. Yesterday before going into work I was really in an unusual mood- somehow angry & frustrated and unable to let out my feelings yet quiet and accepting the way things are. When I got off work, I felt great- just to get out of that place. When I woke up the sun was shining thru a clear blue sky- just great for a day off- the first one I've had since July 16th!

I think your letter really meant a lot because it was as if you really were talking to me. I would love that right now, too.

You know what I said about doing things with other guys- you don't have to explain your relationships with them. Anytime two (or more) people can enjoy each other's presence, it should not be considered wrong for any reason- there's too little caring and appreciation of others in this world. When I was at Lake Geneva, I met a couple of girls who I think are great people and I will probably go up there (I've got to pick up my sisters when they are done with work on August 25) a few days early to enjoy the lake & the people. The kids that work at that camp are a great bunch. But that does not mean you are not my "favoritist" person, because you are. There has never been anyone who has meant so much to me as you do, not even in my family.

Working shifts this summer has kept me from doing very much with my friends from high school. We're all on different shifts or not here or something. So, the guys I talk with most are the ones down at work- and there is not anything worth saying about that. In the last few weeks from working all the time I had lost all ambition, desires, hopes, any thoughts of good things at all. Partly this was because I was so tired. I'll get some of those things back if I know me at all, but I need that vacation too. What makes me sort of sad is thinking that the guys I work with will work their entire lives down there and it will ruin all their ambitions or hopes that they may have had if it has not already.

You said that some people seek out God to find the security and hope they need. Right now, I wish I would believe in God. There are very few things I strongly believe in right now. These last few weeks there were several times I completely lost my temper & cool. I do not do that too often. I think it was because I was so tired but also from feeling frustrated. I want to believe in God, but I can't. I must believe in myself then, and most of the time that is not really enough. I need you because you are the closest person I know. I am only my best when I want to do something for you or with you, not for myself.

> *"My bounty is as boundless as the sea,*
> *My love as deep; the more I give to thee,*
> *The more I have, for both are infinite."*
> —Shakespeare

Quotes seem almost meaningless, yet this really does say what I mean. To me life is fullest and best when I give, not just because I might want to give but because I really need to give to others- it is the only time I feel that I am truly human and mean something. I too want to know you better that I might give you security and the other noble things you spoke of wanting to give me. Our relationship only grows when we learn more about each other and give to each other. I do not want our relationship to only be like a beautiful mountain flower in spring which withers and dies in a day. Even if the flower has a tough time existing, I hope it lasts like a scraggly tree on a barren slope- not always beautiful on the spur-of-the-moment, but beautiful in its strength and endurance. Perhaps it can be both. I do not want you to be a dream either- a dream that I cannot live again.

I too want to thank you for letting me talk to you. If words seem too flowery and meaningless, know that I only try to write what I think inside.

Love, Jeff

On August 7, 1973, Jane wrote

Dear Jeff,

It was 'truly great' to get your letter, too. You said that you were in sort of an angry mood- 'cuz of work and being tired etc. I know what you mean! It seems like some days I am so crabby when I get home and I really have no reason to be. When I am in that sort of mood, I'm not very appreciative toward my parents or anyone. My Grandmother came the other day, and we were talking. She said I should be glad for all I have- a good home & family, an education, enough food & clothes, etc. It's so true, we don't appreciate what we have until we don't have it......."

On July 2, 1974 Jane wrote

Dearest Jeff,

How've you been love? I've missed you so much lately. I too have lost much of my enthusiasm for doing anything.

We have really been busy at work. We are always busy over the fourth of July. I'll probably have to work overtime tomorrow, but it's not too bad. We usually only stay for an hour or two.

My grandmother is here for a week. I drove down to get her- of course my dad was with me.

Tonight, we went to see "The Sound of Music"- for the third time! I think it is really a good movie. It's one of the all-time classics. We all must "Climb our mountains" to find our dreams- they are not easy to come by, we must work for them.

How would you like to have lived in Austria during the war? It would really be a frightening experience. The song "Edelweiss" means so much as far as a love song for a country- a homeland.

I always get all "mushy" over movies like that- especially since it is a love story. It made me think of you and me. What fun we can have with each other, our friends, our home, and children. It's so much fun to be able to live peacefully.

I know this is short. I'm so sleepy and must go to bed. I just wanted to say I love you. I wish you only good things.

Love to you, Jane

On May 30, 1975, near the end of her letter, Jane wrote

…I love you with all my heart. I'm tired of writing how I feel. I must show you and be with you. It's awful to wait. You make me feel so joyful. I don't want to quit writing because then I don't feel so close to you. I'll love you all my life- and I hope it will be a long one.

Love to you, Jane

On July 23, 1975, only a few weeks before our wedding, Jane wrote:

"…. I hope things are going better for you. If not, they will soon.

Yes, I know that we don't have enough money to pay for a lot of the things we want to do. We must talk about that. However, for now I will be satisfied just to be with you. We will take time to do some things when we do have the money.

I need to talk to you about so many things Jeff. It has been a strange time for both of us. Things are changing and we must talk about them. I refuse to let us believe we might have an unhappy life. By god Jeff we are going to make things work for us. We have a very strong and special relationship, and we will not let it fade.

Hang on tight. We have a lot to get through. Much of our time together will be happy. You wait and see. I believe in you and trust you.

I love you, Jane

In a letter that was undated, I wrote-

Jane,

Always remember that I love you with everything that I am. Gibran says that love is a flame that totally consumes the heart yet continually replenishes the heart. Your love is so much. It is what my life is based on and will be based on for the rest of my life. Before you, I never knew that satisfaction I know now. I will always love you. Knowing that you will always love me is the one thing I can depend on right now- there is nothing else I can really be sure of. But no matter what happens I know that you will love me. And that will make my life worth living. You have given me meaning and purpose and that was the one thing last year that I never had…   I know that I love you and that is my one purpose in life. Above all others, and from that flows everything else in my life. I love thinking of you & can see your face now as I write. I love you. Jeff

Chapter Six

MARCH MADNESS

Friday, March 21, 2014

I slept until 4 am. I could not sleep further so I got up.

We went to Jane's appointment with Dr. James Shanks at the Maplewood Cancer Center. A lab tech by the name of Lucy drew Jane's blood and she got it on the first poke from her right antecubital fossa!

When Dr. Shanks came in, he asked about how everything was going.

Then he reviewed the pathology report with us. He had just received the final report that morning. The Mayo clinic pathologist had sent it Wednesday afternoon- but it was not signed out by the pathologist at St. Joseph's Hospital until late Thursday afternoon and faxed to Dr. Shanks this morning.

She has an anaplastic astrocytoma- "at least Grade III".

Dr. Shanks said the Mayo pathologists were usually very definite regarding grading, so he recommended we treat it as grade IV. In other words, it needed to be considered a glioblastoma multiforme type brain cancer, the worst possibility.

He recommended radiation treatment, IMRT (intensity modulated radiation therapy) over 6 weeks (30 fractions) and temozolomide daily during that time and then afterwards 6 cycles 5 days on and 23 days off out of a 28-day cycle. He recommended Dr. Elizabeth Cameron for radiation oncology. She had started working for HealthEast in the fall of 2013. I had had several patients see her for various cancers and all felt she had done a great job. It was not often to get such consistent spontaneous positive feedback from my patients about a specialist. Regarding the oral chemotherapy side effects, Dr. Shanks said that fatigue was common, there was occasional nausea, some decreased white blood cells, and platelets, but that it was not usual to lose a lot of hair. Regarding the radiation treatment, he said that it was common to lose some hair at the site of radiation and that nausea and fatigue were common.

Dr. Shanks asked Jane if she wanted to discuss prognosis. I knew that she did not want to do so but she said yes. She had told me Wednesday night that she was so scared. He said that if it acts more like a Grade 4 cancer, then there was about 1 ½ years median survival. If it acts more like a Grade 3, then there was about 4-5 years median survival.

Bummer!

Even though I had known her prognosis was not good, it was so hard for both of us to hear the reality of what she faced.

Early on the morning of Thursday March 27th, Jane woke me up because she was feeling pain on the right side of her chest. It was only 15 days since she had had her surgery for the brain cancer. She still had to be careful to not move her left arm wrong due to her fractured humerus from that first seizure. She ended up being in different positions at night to try to sleep, so I thought it was probably a muscle cramp. She took some Tylenol, but the pain continued to bother her. I did not want to think the pain could be anything more serious- she had had enough to deal with already. What more could happen?

As a family physician, I know that anytime you have chest pain you have to consider the possibility of pulmonary embolus- blood clot. But in Jane- in my wife?

We both decided that we needed to contact Dr. Julie Vogel, her family physician, to decide what to do. After talking with her, she felt it was best to go to the emergency room to be evaluated. Again. This was getting tiring. But we both got up and dressed and I drove Jane to Woodwinds hospital. She liked it there better. She enjoyed volunteering at the welcome desk at the hospital, knew some of the staff people, and even though St. Joseph's hospital handled more of the specialty type care including the surgery for her brain cancer, she just felt more comfortable at Woodwinds.

In the emergency room, it did not take long for the ER doctor to order a chest CT with contrast to evaluate for a pulmonary embolus. They also did ultrasound of her arms and legs. The ultrasound tech had to be careful when doing the left arm to avoid irritating the humeral fracture site, but efficiently moved through all four extremities. They let me stay by her side while it was done and watch the monitor even though I was not trained to be able to recognize what showed blood clot and what was normal blood flow. I knew that the tech is not supposed to tell us what it looked like to her but wait for the interpretation from the radiologist. We waited for the results. We were both hoping it was normal and we would be able to just go back home.

When the doctor came in to tell us, the look on his face made it plain that it was not negative. Jane had several blood clots in the lung- pulmonary emboli- and blood clots in her right leg and right arm. She had had the PICC line in her right arm after her brain surgery to give the hypertonic saline. She had had the arterial line in her right foot at the time of the surgery and until that was taken out postoperatively could not move her right leg a lot. Both of those are risk factors for clotting, and we later learned that blood clots are common in patients with brain cancer. Dr. Cheema, a partner of Dr. Shanks, later said that up to 25 % of patients with brain cancer can have blood clots.

They recommended that she be transferred to St. Joseph's hospital because if she needed to have an IVC (inferior vena cava) filter placed, that could not be done at Woodwinds Hospital. Also, if she had any bleeding trouble in the brain, she would need to be at St. Joseph's. So, it was arranged that she was transported by ambulance to St. Joseph's hospital and admitted to the neuro ICU on fifth floor. The room she was admitted to was only down the hall from the one she was in after her brain surgery. This room was in the part of the DePaul Tower building that crosses over 10th street in Saint Paul. You could look out the room to the west and see the St. Paul Cathedral. If you walk down the end of the hall and look north, you can see the Minnesota Capitol building where the legislature meets. At night, the lights were shining.

Jane was hurting- every time she breathed, she felt more chest pain on the right side. She was scared. She wanted me to stay with her that night and I wanted to be there with her. We both knew that pulmonary emboli by themselves can be fatal. In the setting of her brain cancer issue, it was certainly an ominous sign. We prayed for healing and for comfort and for peace.

In the ICU room, there is a couch that can convert into a bed by rearranging the pads. That night as I slept, I dreamt of spirits or angels flying over St. Joseph's hospital, taking care of Jane. The following morning on Friday, she already felt better. It did not hurt as much to take a deep breath.

It had been so difficult in the last two weeks to contact everyone in the family as well as close friends to keep them updated. Someone had suggested starting a page on the website Caring Bridge. The hospital had a resource room on the 5th floor that had a computer with connection to the internet as well as chairs for a patient's family member to have a quiet space. There were books and articles regarding various neurologic and cancer conditions. So that Friday March 28th, I started the first entry on Caring Bridge. The college basketball games were going on- it is called March Madness. With all that we had experienced so far, I thought it was an appropriate title to the first entry:

March Madness
Journal entry by Jeff Nelson — 3/28/2014
Jane was feeling fine until she had an episode March 4th when she lost consciousness, fell, broke her left arm, and bruised both of her feet. She was getting worked up to determine the cause when she had a grand mal seizure on the morning of Saturday March 8th, and paramedics took her to Woodwinds Hospital. Multiple scans and multiple consultations ended up showing that she had a lesion in the right side of her brain that looked like a metastatic cancer. However, all the other scans did not show anything. So, she was scheduled for and had brain surgery on March 12th at St Joseph's Hospital in St. Paul by Dr. Richard Gregory. It was found that she has a primary brain tumor- that is, it started in the brain. It could not all be removed, because there would have been increased risk of leaving her paralyzed. She got home on Saturday March 15th and had been gradually progressing. Her arm fracture is healing and feeling better, and hopefully next week she can get out of the sling that she has needed. Her feet swelling and bruising have been improving. We saw her oncologist, Dr James Shanks last Friday and for her situation radiation and chemotherapy is recommended and she is scheduled to see the radiation oncologist next week.

Then yesterday morning when she woke up, she had pain on the right side of her chest that persisted, and she also felt somewhat short of breath. So, we went to Woodwinds hospital ER and it was determined that she has several small blood clots in her right lung- or pulmonary emboli. She has a blood clot in her right leg and her right arm, and she was started on a blood thinner. They must be careful though because of the recent surgery. So, she is back at St Joseph's Hospital in St. Paul for the treatment, and to be prepared if there are any complications from the blood thinning therapy. She is feeling better today. We will hope that she just continues to make good progress.

We had found out last Friday that her tumor is an anaplastic astrocytoma, at least grade 3- and they are recommending that it be treated as a grade 4 due to the details. So, we ask for your continued prayers. We have appreciated the amazing support from family and friends as she is going through this.

Chapter Seven

CHRIST THE KING LUTHERAN CHURCH

Jane and I were married at Christ the King Lutheran Church in Bloomington, Minnesota on August 2, 1975. This was the congregation where she had been confirmed. She told a story of having to wait a long time for her dad to pick her up after confirmation at least one time. It was a drive from their home in Burnsville. Whether her dad had forgotten, or got tied up doing something else, I do not know. But I know that when she was tired of being patient about something, it was one of the stories that she would mention- having to be patient waiting for her father.

Her parents continued to worship there until they transferred to Prince of Peace Lutheran Church in Burnsville. In that summer of 1975, they were still members at Christ the King and so that was where we were married. Pastor Milo Englestad performed the ceremony. Joel Hendrickson, my college roommate for 2 years, was my best man. Jane's sister Sandra was the maid of honor. Jane's brother, David and our brother-in-law, Lou Behensky (Sandra's husband) were groomsmen for me. My sisters, Nancy and Janet, were bridesmaids for Jane. I remember it as such a happy day. I look back at our wedding photos, and it was a joy. I remember that I smiled so much that day that my facial muscles were literally sore – aching from being tired.

We had the reception at Jane's parents' home in Burnsville- at 2201 S. Skyline Drive. It was a small reception and the wedding cost less than $500.

But it was such a celebration, and we were both so happy. When Jane threw the bouquet she had, her friend and former college roommate Kathy caught it- all the girls were jumping trying to catch it. When I threw Jane's garter, the guys did not have the same energy!

When we left their home that evening, we drove to the hotel in Bloomington -The Registry-for our first night of our honeymoon. Because of working for Northwest Airlines, several of Jane's high school friends were able to reserve a room at a discount for us and gave that to us as their wedding present. When we got there and checked in and they gave us the key to the room, Jane and I thought a mistake had been made. We had the presidential suite!!! It was huge. The bedroom itself was much larger than the usual hotel room. I remember looking in the shower and there were 5 nozzles that directed water- one from each side wall and one from the ceiling! We called back to her parent's home and thought everyone should come up to see it! But no one did and we had the rest of the evening and night to ourselves. It was a wonderful beginning to a wonderful life together.

The next day we drove up to Brainerd to a place called Grand View Lodge that was at the north end of Gull Lake. I had seen an ad for it in some magazine and thought it looked like a fun place to do our honeymoon. Little did I know how much over the years it would become a family tradition. We swam in the lake. We did some kayaking. We could play tennis on the courts and golf on the 9-hole course, but we mostly enjoyed our time together and relaxed. Oh, and the food at Grand View is great!

After our honeymoon, we drove from her parent's home down to Iowa City, Iowa where I was starting medical school. We lived in Iowa City from August of 1975 to June of 1979.

For residency in family medicine, I went to St. Paul Ramsey Hospital in St. Paul from July 1, 1979 until June 30, 1982. While I was in my first year, Jane had Chris in March of 1980- our first child- born at St. Paul Ramsey.

We felt like we should get Chris baptized even though we were not attending church on any regular basis. Pastor Milo Englestad was still at Christ the King in Bloomington and Chris was baptized there. It was the beginning of our thinking of finding a church home, but residency was too busy to think much about anything except work and family.

It was August 2, 2015- our 40th wedding anniversary- that we next attended a service at Christ the King. Jane had had her brain cancer since

March of 2014. Our 40th anniversary was one of the landmark events in life. I remember that when we went to the service, we received communion. Jane had her left hemiparesis- her left arm and leg weakness- but walked up to take communion with me. We held hands as we walked up together. I had tears in my eyes as I saw her receive communion. We took pictures of each other outside the church.

Chapter Eight

SWEET DETERMINATION

Jane took two summer school classes in 1975 at Luther College after finishing her junior year there. She also wrote her senior paper that summer.

After we were married at Christ the King Lutheran Church in Bloomington, and after our honeymoon at Grand View Lodge, we moved to Iowa City, Iowa, where I began medical school at the University of Iowa. Luther College allowed her to take her last required classes at the University of Iowa that fall. Luther allowed her to transfer those credits back so that she could graduate from Luther with her B.A. degree in biology.

We had borrowed money from my parents to help cover the cost of that fall semester at the University of Iowa. In early 1976, we had no income, had basically run out of money, and could not and did not want to borrow any more from our parents. Jane was doing her best to get a job but that was not a quick process. We applied for and were approved to receive food stamps. Neither of us liked needing to do this, but we were always grateful for the support of society. Ever since we have been happy to pay our taxes to support others in need. We wanted our tax dollars to be well spent, but we knew that we have been blessed.

Jane found her first full-time year-round job as a research assistant at the University of Iowa- in neurobiochemistry working for a Dr. Gal whose office and research lab were in the old psychiatry hospital of the medical school campus. She started her job there on April 12, 1976. She quickly found out that he was a tyrant- he would verbally abuse people, putting them down. My sweet hardworking loving wife would come home in tears with how she was treated at times. Many other employees of Dr. Gal would leave his employment within a day, or a week, or a month. But Jane was concerned she would have difficulty getting another job if she quit too quickly and knew that we needed the income to survive.

I did not push her to stay because I hated to see how it hurt her so many days to work in that environment. Their research was on biopterin, a chemical that is involved in some neural pathways in the mammalian brain. She toughed it out for one entire year. Then she quit that job when she got another that was in the physiology department. She was assisting a Dr. Dave Dawson do research on cell membrane transport using the bladder wall of various species to study the effect of amiloride among other studies. She continued to work there until I finished medical school in May of 1979, and we moved to the St. Paul area for my residency which started in late June.

Those years were my first exposure to the quiet strength and determination that she had. What a wonderful companion.

We have been blessed over the years to have many wonderful pastors at our church. Pastor Joel Bexell called on our home in Cottage Grove sometime in late 1982. He was so welcoming as were other members that we decided to begin worshiping at St. Luke Lutheran in Cottage Grove and had Tom baptized there after his birth in early 1983. We had both been raised in Lutheran churches in what became the ELCA synod (Evangelical Lutheran Church in America). Over the years all three of our children were confirmed at St. Luke Lutheran. We developed many friendships there. Jane taught Sunday school and after a number of years ended up serving as the Sunday school superintendent as well as serving on the church council.

By the time that Jane had developed her brain cancer, our associate pastor was Pastor Amanda Olson de Castillo. In early August 2014, Jane had written the following e-mail to Pastor Amanda in response to a sermon that she had given.

Jane's approach to this situation is another example of the sweet determination that she had in dealing with problems in life. She knew that God loved her even if she could not be spared from the tragedies of life. She knew that there is more to life than only this physical existence.

From: Jane Nelson <janenelson9215@gmail.com>
Date: August 4, 2014 at 8:49:34 AM CDT
To: Pastor Amanda <pr.amanda@stlukecg.com >
Subject: Thanks

Pastor Amanda,

I wanted to thank you for your sermon on racing and how you prepared yourself for each event. As I go through this cancer race, I found it helpful to hear about your winning attitude and visualizing your route and winning at the end. Although my prognosis is not very good, I know that I will win the race because God loves me and will be there as I cross the finish line.

I have an MRI this morning and results tomorrow and my mantra will be that I can do this because I am strong, and I will win because God loves me.

Thank you for your help. I pray for positive results.!

Jane Nelson

Here is the response that Pastor Amanda sent to Jane.

From: Amanda Olson de Castillo <Pr.Amanda@StLukeCG.com>
Date: August 5, 2014 at 3:29:36 PM CDT
To: Jane Nelson <janenelson9215@gmail.com>
Subject: RE: Thanks

Jane,

I pray that God continues to bless and keep you in this cancer race that you are in the midst of. As I read what you wrote below, the words from Hebrews 12:1 came to mind, "Therefore, since we are surrounded by such a great cloud of witnesses, let us throw off everything that hinders and the sin that so easily entangles, and let us run with perseverance the race marked out for us. Let us fix our eyes on Jesus."

I am thankful that you do have many faithful witnesses in your life as you yourself are a faithful witness. To be reminded that God will be there not only as you cross the finish line one day, but also has been with you today as you received the MRI results is a comfort, and sometimes the only comfort, in the midst of all that occurs.

You have been in my prayers for months already, and in God's hands for even longer. Today my prayer has been for the results that you received to be good results.

Should you like to connect for a visit, I am here for that reason.

In Christ,

Pr. Amanda

"Hope does not disappoint us, because God has poured out his love into our hearts by the Holy Spirit, whom he has given us." Romans 5:5

Chapter Nine

JANE'S GIFTS

Jane Marie Korsrud Nelson Resume
Creative artist-floral design
Great chef
Experienced wedding coordinator
Seamstress supreme
Master gardener
Domestic engineer
Counselor
Biologist
Teacher
Amazing smell ability
Master cake decorator
Creative artist- crafts & cross stitch
Golfer
Loving daughter
Loving sister
Loving sister-in-law
Wonderful lover
Wonderful mother
Wonderfully patient wife

Going rate for her services—beyond my means.
She blesses us with the gift of her time
As she knows that God first blessed her.

Chapter Ten

JANE'S CHILDHOOD

Jane wrote the below on February 27, 1978:

I want so much to write a book about my life-my feelings, my thoughts, my likes, and dislikes- but I lack the determination to actually sit down and do it. I am hoping that my writing will help future generations to understand what it was like to grow up and live during my lifetime. I feel that it is very important for us to know how others think and live not only to benefit our lives but also to enjoy reading about life as it existed in the '60s & '70s. With this in mind, I hope that I can find the motivation to complete this work.

I was born on Dec. 16, 1953 in Pipestone, Mn. My dad tells me that it was a very cold day and that it was snowing. Mom went into the hospital about a month before I was to be born so that my birth could be induced. Since my brother David was born by Caesarean section, they wanted me to be born before I got too big to be born without a section. Mom was Rh negative, so they were ready to transfuse my blood in case anything went wrong. Fortunately, everything went okay.

At times I think I can remember things from my early childhood, but I don't know. It could be that I am just recalling what my folks have told me. I seem to remember calling people up on the phone without knowing who I was calling. In those days to call someone you just lifted the receiver and gave the operator a number. One time when I called a man answered. I was a really mischievous child. Until I was two years old, I cried an awful lot. Mom says she and Dad used to rock me all night trying to get me to sleep. They took me to the doctor, and he said that perhaps I had an advanced nervous system. When I was older, I used to get into trouble all the time. I got more spankings. I broke the neighbors milk bottles, threw toys out of a neighbor's window while at a coffee party with Mom, got into the cow pasture in our backyard and rubbed manure all over myself, sprayed the neighbor kids with a hose- among an assortment of other things. A lot of my adventures were done with the aid of my brother and Alison Ronning- a friend of ours. We were three little white-haired kids who looked cute but did devilish things. David cut off my hair once and threw my toy china dishes down the clothes chute. We all ran off to the drugstore once and some man brought us home in his car. At nights I can remember I thought there were bugs crawling all over the drapes in our bedroom. All three of us kids slept in the same bedroom. Sandra's bed was by the window and when I slept with her, I could always see the bugs on the curtains. It seemed so real to me. The girl who lived upstairs in our house, Paula, had some stilts that she kept by the front steps.

When I was four, we moved to Bloomington, Mn. From then on, my memory gets much better. Sandra, David & I stayed at Grandmas while the moving was done.

We liked to play in the dirt piles made by the graders in the backyard. Our back yard was huge and bowl shaped. The house was a 3 bedroom with a walkout basement. We didn't have a garage. My best friend, Heidi Hoffmann, lived 2 doors down Vincent Avenue. We played "horses" a lot. One of us was a horse and one was the rider. We also liked to play baseball and hopscotch.

When I started kindergarten, Heidi went with me. We walked to the Methodist church for school. On our way we had to cross "Mr. Green-man's" yard. (He lived in a green house). He was "always" in a bad mood and we thought he was a mean man because he yelled at us for walking in his yard.

During the winter Mr. Hoffman made a skating rink in their back yard and I learned to ice skate there. I took my play folding chair out to hold in front of me so I wouldn't fall down. I liked to be outside. We also went sliding a lot in the snow. When we had to be inside, we played downstairs. We made a playhouse underneath the basement stairs.

I went to Washburn Elementary school for 1st grade. We had to take the bus. School was divided into shifts and I was in the morning shift which met from ~7:00 a.m. to ~12:30 p.m. My teacher's name was Miss Weingartner. She appeared to be really nice when I first met her, but I ended up hating her. I blame her some for my future attitude towards school. She was very strict with us. If we talked during class, she pinned a big yellow sign on our chest saying, "I will not talk during class." I was so afraid that I would have to wear a sign. You had to wear it all day and even wear it home. It really scared me. I think I might have had to wear a sign once during the year but I'm not certain. A lot of times when I was young and did something wrong, I was so mad that I got punished because I really didn't feel that I was doing anything wrong. I didn't mean to be bad. Finger painting was my funnest favorite activity. I had my 1st test, a spelling test. I was scared but was surprised to find it so easy. I got 100 on it.

For second grade I moved to Creekside school and Miss Cotter was my teacher. I enjoyed second grade. I can remember that when we had dancing, I always had to dance with a real fat boy. Joy Watson, a friend, always got to dance with the boy I wanted- the most handsome in the class of course. It seemed like I always got stuck with the duds. Sometimes I couldn't believe my luck- or bad luck I should say. We used to write a lot of stories in that class. The teacher would pick a few students to write a story on the black board. I had to write really small so I could get all of my story in. When we wrote on paper, we always drew an accompanying picture to illustrate the story. I frequently wrote about my family. If I didn't know how to spell a word, I would draw it right in line with the sentence. We had a hamster who ate cabbage, and I didn't know how to spell cabbage, so I drew it instead.

My birthday and Christmas, along with summer vacations were my favorite times of the year. I got so excited at Christmas I would actually shake. I always peeked at my presents because I just couldn't wait for Christmas. We opened our presents on Christmas eve. We had Christmas at Grandma's in Austin, Mn. Aunt Shirley would sneak outside and ring the doorbell pretending to be Santa Claus. We would never see her do it. We constantly looked out the front window to try to see Santa. After the doorbell rang, we would rush out to Grandmas porch and find clothes baskets full of presents. It was so exciting- we had a hard time waiting for Christmas eve dinner and the dishes to be done so that we could open our presents. I always liked to get dolls best.

We'd always put up our Christmas tree right before my birthday. I'd have all my neighborhood friends over for cake & ice cream. We played a few games like dropping clothespins in a milk bottle or "pin the tail on the donkey."

The summer before 3rd grade we built a house in Burnsville, Mn just south of Bloomington. Dad finished the inside of the house himself and we spent several weekends painting and puttying nail holes. (I mostly puttied.) Our yard and the road in front of the house were dirt and turned to mud when it rained. I spent much of the next few years wearing boots. It was fun moving into a new house. Sandra and I shared a "huge" bedroom. The most fascinating feature of the house, at least to David and me was the radio-intercom. Each room had a speaker, and we had a great time talking back & forth.

Before each school year began, we got to go shopping for new clothes. I especially liked to get new shoes. Shiny black patent leathers were my favorite. When I was in Pipestone, I got some new shoes and had to wear them to bed I liked them so much. Dad has always been an ardent "money-saver". For new shoes we always had to go to this rundown house where this old man sold cheap off-brand shoes. I hated it. I got a pair of black patent leathers, but they weren't "real" patent leather and not half as shiny as I'd hoped. I used to rub them with Vaseline every night to make them shinier. I would dream about getting new shoes.

Chapter Eleven

RADIATION AND OTHER HAPPENINGS

"Any day that is not scary is a good day."

Today is April 2, 2014. The above is what Jane said after supper tonight. Chris stayed with her today- he works from home on Wednesdays so he can be with her and help. She had further episodes of the chest feeling going up to her throat and difficulty talking. Each episode usually lasted less than half a minute but was frightening because she did not know what was going on. Dr Hungs thinks these are a form of seizure and when she had talked to his nurse yesterday (while we were at Dr Cameron's office) he recommended that she increase her Keppra to 1000 mg twice a day.

The thought of those episodes being seizures was frightening to both of us after all that she has gone thru.

Dr Cameron did another CT of her head yesterday to make sure there was no sign of bleeding that could be causing those episodes. Her plan was to start radiation therapy on Thursday April 10th. There needs to be sufficient healing of the tissues after brain surgery before radiation is usually started.

What Jane said tonight made me think about all the people that have something scary happen to them. Women or children who are abused, someone who loses their job, someone diagnosed with a serious illness like Jane has had to deal with in these last few weeks--- having a day where nothing scary happens is a good day.

Today is Friday, April 4th, and Jane and I are both hoping that we can just have some quiet time together this weekend to rest. It has been exhausting. I did not sleep well last night. Why is it that I sleep better on most nights before working at the clinic, and then on a night before a day I do not have to work at the clinic, I often sleep the worst of the week? Is it the accumulated stress of what happens during Monday thru Thursday and too much input in my brain?

At any rate, it looked like a nap in the afternoon would be nice. Jane wanted to call Dr Hungs office to let them know that her episodes were not any better since increasing the Keppra dose to 1000 mg twice a day. When I called, at first the receptionist said that Dr Hungs wanted to see Jane and offered an appointment next week. I said that we needed to talk to his nurse and not wait that long. She transferred us to his nurse- I think it was Darcy- and explained there was no change in the frequency of the episodes, and she said that Dr Hungs wanted to see Jane and offered either 11:15 or 1:00 as appointment times. I knew that we needed to go in, but I knew that Jane was exhausted and would not want to go after all the emotions of yesterday.

On Thursday April 3rd, she had the "mapping" done. She had the molding of the face mask that is used to hold her head in place during radiation therapy. That did very much give the feeling of claustrophobia but thankfully did not last too long. When she had the MRI with contrast following that, she said that she imagined that she was on the floaties up at the lake- Sarah had encouraged her to use that image to help relax. That was the perfect thought, as it has always been so relaxing for her to do that. So, it helped her get thru that part of the day. She did not have to take any relaxer medication. She had been so afraid that she was not going to be able to do it. After all she had been thru, I had thought this would go ok, but I had never experienced it and did not know what the mask formation was like. But I also know how much someone can be affected by fatigue, and Jane was exhausted from the poor sleep this last week on top of all the earlier problems.

So now this morning on Friday, the thought of having to go to another doctor's appointment was intolerable when she was hoping to have one day of not doing that. She was angry and shouted out she did not want to go to the appointment with Dr Hungs. My gentle, quiet, loving wife was not herself. I made the appointment for 11:15 so we could just get done with it. She did not want to go but knew that she had to do so.

I went out to snow blow the driveway. There had been at least 4 inches of heavy wet snow overnight. Thankfully the snowblower worked, and when I got done, I took my shower, and Jane was ready. We drove to Neurologic Associates in Maplewood to see Dr. Hungs. He is always so pleasant and understanding. After talking with her, he said he was sure that her episodes were "little seizures" and recommended that she start taking Vimpat which was a newer medication that had worked well and had little risk of side effects. He said he had checked and that it was Tier 2 for our insurance, but that if it were not covered, we could use another medication. He wrote out prescriptions for it, and we were out of his office within about a half an hour.

We stopped at Bakers Square to get a French silk pie and drove back to Cottage Grove. We stopped at Walgreens to drop off the prescription. Then we went to the clinic to get Jane's INR done. That is the test to make sure her blood thinning is the correct amount. When someone is on warfarin or the trade name Coumadin, the INR test is done on a regular basis even long term because many things affect that, including what you eat. We went to Culver's to get some lunch, to the bank to get some cash, and back to Walgreens to pick up the Vimpat. Then we went home. In all it took about 2 1/2 hours to do all the above, and we felt that was pretty good. We were both able to get some rest that afternoon. In the evening we watched part of the movie "The Best Exotic Marigold Hotel" with Judi Dench, Bill Nye, Tom Wilkinson, and Maggie Smith. It was very funny, but we were so tired that we watched about half of it and then went to bed. Jane's INR was 3.1, and Dr Vogel said we could stop the Lovenox- no more shots! - and take warfarin 2 mg per day Friday Saturday Sunday and get an INR on Monday, April 7th.

That Monday I was working at the clinic when I was paged to call Dr. Cameron.

She had already talked with Jane and wanted to let me know that the MRI with contrast on Thursday had shown significant uptake surrounding the area of surgery. There had been no enhancement on the postsurgical MRI with contrast done on March 15th at St. Joseph's on the day Jane was discharged home after the brain surgery by Dr. Gregory. Dr. Cameron had reviewed it with several other specialists and was concerned that the tumor was already growing. She wanted to have Jane start her radiation therapy early-the next day Tuesday 4/8 instead of waiting till the planned Thursday 4/10. She said we would still wait till 4/10 to start the oral chemotherapy. She wanted to talk with us further on Tuesday when Jane got the first treatment.

We continue to hope for Jane to heal well and do well. Each time something like this happens, it is so hard. I cried at the clinic as I was telling Jodi Robinson that I needed to schedule out Tuesday afternoon 4/8 so that I could be with Jane for that appointment.

The radiation therapy itself was not hard to tolerate. Jane had a variety of friends and family take her for her treatments when I was working at the clinic. I requested reducing my schedule to half time to be with Jane more as well as to take her to the many appointments and that was approved. I have worked at the clinic for 32 years at this point, and I wanted to spend as much time with Jane as I could, not knowing what the future would bring. When I worked on Mondays, Sarah would spend the day with Jane. She would come Sunday night and sleep over at the house, since I went to work early on Monday morning. Fortunately, her job had allowed her to change her schedule to work four 10-hour days on Tuesday thru Friday and have Monday each week to be able to help us out. I would be home on Tuesdays. Then Chris was able to be with Jane on Wednesday as he could work from home that day each week. Tom likewise was able to adjust his schedule so that he could be with her on Thursday until I got home from the clinic. Jane's friends helped at times as well.

During this same time, Jane's mother had the evaluation for her postmenopausal bleeding that started the same day that Jane had her first seizure. Pelvic ultrasound followed by endometrial biopsy showed that Helen had a grade 1 endometrial adenocarcinoma. That is, she had uterine cancer. But fortunately, it was expected that a hysterectomy would likely cure her condition. Hopefully, she would tolerate the surgery and heal well. I was hoping that would be the case for Jane's sake as well as her mother's sake.

In my diary on May 10th, I wrote "This morning my hope and prayer is that Jane and I and all of our family learn to not fear "death"- the end of life on this earth, but at the same time learn to make the most of every moment that we have in this life."

Jane finished her course of 30 radiation treatments on Tuesday May 20th.

Chapter Twelve

WEDDINGS

During the summer of June thru August of 2014, Jane kept a diary of some of her thoughts. On June 7th she wrote:

"The wedding <u>will</u> go well. It <u>will</u> be a happy day. I <u>will</u> make it thru the weekend. What a blessing to be here to enjoy today. Linda & I are going shoe shopping. I need to find something else to do besides watching tv. Help me Lord. Help me to not have any more seizures or bladder infections. Help me to tolerate the chemo & have a good time at the cabin. Calm my fears. Give me lots of days and years. I love you."

A good part of the following is from my diary:

I am writing this on Tuesday July 1st, 2014. Saturday was a special day.

Tom & Darcy had their wedding at Wooddale Lutheran Church in St Louis Park and Pastor Tim Rauk presided at the wedding. Darcy was a beautiful bride and Tom a handsome groom and the ceremony was very special. Jane felt better on Saturday than she had felt since all her cancer issues got started. She and I walked down the aisle on each side of Tom and that was a special feeling. Darcy's mom- Mariann- walked her down the aisle since her father is in a wheelchair and could not do so.

Her sister Angie Gutierrez was her maid of honor and Angie's children Victoria and Lucas were the flower girl and the ringbearer. Sarah was one of the bridesmaids as well as Kelsey Oakey, Diane Tolzmann, and Christina Hausman. Tom had Chris be his best man, and his groomsmen were Josh Dwyer, Peter Van Hoven, Dave Olson, and Justin LaCroix.

Will Zylstra, the younger son of my sister Janet, videotaped the service for us with our camcorder as he had done at Sarah and Jake's wedding 3 years ago. Pastor Rauk noted that Angie and her husband Victor had been married there at Wooddale Lutheran 10 years ago on the same day.

Tom & Darcy planted a tree for their unity ceremony and had got dirt from both our yard as well as Westermann's yard to pour on the soil of their tree that they are going to plant in their front yard. They had a friend play the violin for the processional- Jesu, Joy of Man's Desiring- and it was done beautifully.

It rained hard about 45 minutes before the service. It was a true downpour. Some people coming into the church could not help but get drenched. It also rained after the service. The reception was being held at the Hope Glenn farm in Cottage Grove. Our plan after the wedding service was for me to drive Jane back home and then I would go on to the reception. Jane would be able to rest a little and then our neighbor Dick Lippert was going to drive her to the reception.

As Jane and I drove from the church back home it was pouring rain so hard that at times it was difficult to see the roadway. The wipers were going as fast as they could and there were still times that it was hard to see. I almost had to pull off the road, but I was worried that we had more chance of being hit by someone else on the road who could not see where they were going. There was also lightning and thunder. Jane was anxious even before this weather. But as we were driving, she had a full-blown panic attack. She said that we needed to call the owner of Hope Glenn to postpone the reception. She did not see how anyone was going to go to the reception in these kinds of conditions. I told her it was not our decision to do that.

Having it rain hard was Jane's worst nightmare for the reception given its outdoor location etc. When we had first visited Hope Glen with Tom and Darcy in March of 2013 when they were looking at prospective reception sites, both Jane and I thought that they should consider another site. At that time, the only building was a barn which could not hold the number of people that Tom and Darcy planned to invite to their wedding. The open sided pavilion where their guests ate dinner was not built at that time, nor were the separate small buildings that contained the bathrooms. In 2013, Jane and I did not see how it would be a venue that would work for some individuals such as Darcy's father who was wheelchair bound. But with the structures that were built by June of 2014, it did work out.

The ushers and groomsmen used umbrellas to help all get from their cars to the barn or pavilion. They formed a line of umbrellas when it was time to go from the barn up the steps to the pavilion for dinner. Some friends of ours, Dave and Nancy Pawlik, brought their RV so that when Jane got tired, she was able to rest in the RV and not have to go home.

The food was good- chicken, beef, potato salad, broccoli salad, fresh fruit, etc. The cake tasted good. It was also the birthday of Tom's friend Justin as well as one of Darcy's relatives. About 9 pm the rain stopped. A little later there was a rainbow over the pavilion that was an exceptionally large, wide rainbow- so beautiful!

After dinner was done, Angie gave a short speech as maid of honor, Chris gave a speech as best man, and Darcy had asked me to give one on behalf of the parents since her dad could not and her mom was uncomfortable in front of crowds. Jane, Mariann, and I were standing at the front opposite where the microphone was listening to Angie and Chris, and then Mariann and I walked together, and I gave a short one that went something like this-

Wayne, Mariann, Jane, and I want to welcome you. We thank you for sharing this special day with us. We are blessed to have Tom & Darcy in our families.

We celebrate the lives of Tom and Darcy and the lives of family and friends that we get to share time with.

The weather and rain tonight remind me of a saying that I first heard in the last several months- "Life isn't about waiting for the storm to pass; it is about learning to dance in the rain." I hope you will enjoy dancing with Tom and Darcy later.

There is a saying that I would like to share with you that I heard from Pastor Joel Bexell who often used it at the end of services at St. Luke's.

"As you go on your way,
May God go with you.
May he go before you to show you the way,
Behind you to encourage you,
Beside you to befriend you,
Above you to watch over you, and
Within you to give you peace."
Let's celebrate Tom & Darcy and enjoy the rest of the evening together!

One picture that I have from that evening is one of Tom and Jane dancing together. Both look so happy as Jane is looking up into Tom's eyes. She is wearing her orange dress and orange sweater and her dark navy blue tennis shoes with bright orange shoelaces. I was thankful that she had decided to wear comfortable shoes that would not cause her to have foot pain during that time. She is laughing and so happy and so proud as she dances with Tom.

Only 3 days following the wedding, Jane's mother Helen had her hysterectomy for the uterine cancer. She had delayed the procedure because she wanted to make sure that she would be at Tom and Darcy's wedding. Fortunately, the surgery went well, and Helen recovered as well as an 86-year-old woman can be expected to do. I only wish that Jane had such a treatable and curable cancer. I know that Jane, her parents, and all our family wished that were the case as well.

Weddings were always special for Jane. She worked as a wedding coordinator at our church for around 11 years from 1995-2006. She did it so well, that after a while, our pastors would have her do the rehearsals at times, so they did not have to spend Friday evening as well as Saturday with the wedding party. Pastors and their families do need some time together! Jane would talk about how different bridegrooms and brides would behave and say that it was easy to see the couples that were truly in love with each other by how they behaved both during the rehearsal as well as the wedding service. I wish that every couple could experience the love that Jane and I have experienced during our marriage.

In our family our oldest son Chris was the first to be married to Julie Greene in July of 2004. Because they were living in St. Paul and Julie was from the Oakland, California area, they decided they wanted to get married in the St. Paul area. They decided to have the ceremony at our church- St. Luke Lutheran- in Cottage Grove and the reception at the Southview Country Club where Chris had worked as a bartender part-time. Jane loved being able to help Chris and Julie plan their wedding. She made the flower arrangements that were used in the church for the ceremony. It was so emotional for both Jane and I to see our oldest child getting married to such a wonderful woman. Chris and Julie looked very happy together.

Our daughter Sarah was married to Jacob Danner in July of 2011 and Jane especially loved the planning for their wedding since it is traditional for the bride and her mom to do a lot of the wedding planning and so Jane did not have to worry about being too involved. We are blessed to have such a wonderful son-in-law as Jake. I had not realized that Sarah had thought for some time that it would be fun to have her wedding at Grand View Lodge where we had spent many family vacations. We have so many wonderful memories of family time together in the Brainerd Lakes area including at Grand View. I was concerned that it would cost more to have a wedding there and that it would involve even more traveling for family members as well as guests. But I was so proud of Sarah and Jake and Jane as the specific plans developed. Grand View was a beautiful location to have Sarah and Jake's wedding, and it was actually less expensive than it would have been in the Twin Cities. One of the fun planning activities was trying out different types of cake that were made by Jackie Tyrrell who had her small specialty baking company in the Brainerd area. What wonderful cake! I so remember Sarah and Jake and Jane and I going to her place to sample the options for the wedding cake. That is such a tough job for the father of the bride-to-be!

But I must come back to the reality of the summer of 2014. Jane had difficulties with recurrent bladder infections and minor seizures and a variety of things that just made it difficult to enjoy daily life. Part of her difficulties were related to the oral chemotherapy that she needed to take- temozolomide. Her appetite would go down significantly for days after her monthly course of medication among other things. She had a follow up brain MRI on August 4th.

That day she wrote in her diary-

"I hope and pray that the results of the MRI are good. Help me dear Lord. Give me your miracle and your peace. Help me to feel your love. I feel like you want me to do something here on earth yet. I love you dear Lord. Hear the prayers of my family and friends. Help me to be strong & full of joy & excitement tomorrow.

I love you."

I do not think Jane was aware how much she taught all of us faith, hope, love, patience, and so much more.

On August 21st she wrote "Friends truly are the best medicine. I see God's work in each and every one of them." We spent a week up north with our friends the Valencours and the Stoners and very much enjoyed our time together.

Judy Williams Farrell was a close friend of Jane's growing up. Her oldest child, her son Doug, was getting married in Provincetown, Massachusetts to his fiancé Lynn Sarcione on Saturday, September 20th. Over the summer, Jane and I had hesitated to make plans to go to the wedding with the ongoing difficulty she had with seizures and other issues.

But we both decided that it was best to try to go and handle it as well as we could. Our flight landed in Boston about 8 p.m. on Friday, September 19th. We rented a car and drove the lengthy trip down to the base of Cape Cod and back up to Provincetown where the wedding would be held. The Provincetown Inn was already booked up when we scheduled our flight, so we stayed at the Inn at the Moors a short distance away.

Saturday morning, we met our friends Jody and Evers outside the Provincetown Inn and walked around town quite a bit- walked to the house that Judy and her husband Bruce had rented for their family to stay at for the wedding. But they were not there, so we sat on their patio for a while. Then we called Judy and found out that she and her family were just starting a Trolley ride tour of Provincetown. We walked back downtown and saw them on the tour. We ate lunch at Betty's Bayside restaurant with Jody and Evers. Later, we saw Judy and Bruce as well as Judy's sister Sue on our way back to the hotel.

The wedding was at 4 p.m.- it was a beautiful day for an outdoor wedding.

Jane and Judy and Jody had been best friends in high school, and it was wonderful for them to be together to celebrate the marriage of Judy's son. Jane and I stayed several more days in the Cape Cod area before returning home. I remember a moment while we were staying at the Ocean Club hotel on Smuggler's beach in South Yarmouth. We had enjoyed the day and were resting together on the bed and suddenly Jane had a minor seizure with the sensation in her throat and lips and chest. All the peace we had felt just vanished and the anxiety level rose. We were both still learning how to deal with all of this.

Chapter Thirteen

GNO TRIP TO FLORIDA AND COMING HOME

Jane's group of high school friends "GNO" "Girls Night Out" group- had continued to get together on a regular basis all these years since high school. Sometimes only a few of them could get together. Sometimes when one member that was living in another state came for a visit, they would all get together. When everyone was there, they had twelve in the group- Jane, Jody Arman-Jones, Judy Williams Farrell, Carol Minerich Ford, Margaret Hammer Hinke, Suzie Reynolds Bartell, Debbie Almquist Morgan, Jadelle Berthe Breitbarth, Marcia Neumann Marti, Cindy Buker McConnell, Sandy Carson King, and Lynn Moriarty Lawrence. Jane was the first one to turn 60 when she had her birthday on December 16, 2013. Over the following year the rest of the group had their 60th birthdays.

They had gone on a cruise when they turned 50, had stayed at a home in North Carolina for a week when they turned 55, and they had scheduled a week together on Captiva Island in Florida for November 2014. They were able to have 11 of the 12 go on this trip. Jane was bound and determined that she was going to go no matter what. Sometimes I thought she seemed to use her left leg just a little differently. I had wanted her to get an MRI before she went on the trip to make sure there was nothing new going on that would increase the risk for her. But I knew that she did not want to do this, and it was useless to try to press the issue. She and Jody flew down together on Saturday November 8th. The group rented a house that was right on the beach and had a swimming pool. They made many of their meals right there at the house.

It was the custom that each member of the group gave a gift to the rest to commemorate their time together and their friendship at these five-year reunions. One of those gifts that year was a small 4x6 pocketbook. It had slots to put in cards etc. and a floral design on the cover, and inside the cover was the name of the member. The next page had a saying- "A true friend is someone who reaches for your hand and touches your heart." (Unknown author). In Jane's book, the next two pages had pictures of Jane from their school years together. The following pages had a picture of the group from their 40-year-old reunion and their 55-year-old reunion. But the reason that I include all of this is that the following pages were ones where the group gave each other feedback.

I have included a few to share some of their thoughts about Jane.

Things I like about you...

your strength and gentle
determination.
your truthfulness; the soft spoken
way you share your honest opinions
your quiet chuckle when something
tickles you.

that you're a loyal and true
friend.

Your quiet, gentle, beautiful spirit.
Yet your strength and determination
now shining through.

Everything! Your kindness,
The calming way you approach
things. Your wonderful way
with words and expressing
yourself. Your impishness and
the sparkle
in your eyes.
Your strength
and bravery

I have always thought of you as kind the matriarch of this group - maybe because you are the oldest. You always seemed so wise and able to direct us. You always put the pictures together! When I was way younger (and still) I always thought you were, so pretty and smart and nice and how lucky I was to have you as a friend. If God chooses to take you before me (which I pray he will not) I will find a way to continue with wonderful memories but there will always be a hole in my heart that will never be filled.

Jane, when I first met you I loved being around you because you just radiated calm and composure. Your family, when I would pick you up was always that way, so calm, quiet, serene. And then you built your family the same way.

Now as you face this challenge ahead, you are helping each and everyone of us in GNO to face the world with that same calm and serene strength. Because of you we will all be better and stronger as we face the future.

I'll Never Forget . . . . Jane

- How you are so intelligent and yet never made any of us feel stupid
- How you are the great diplomat of the group and over the years I think you helped to prevent any mini-wars between women as various subjects were discussed!
- Fun at all the slumber parties!
- Celebrating 40 at Neuman's Cabin
  55 at Kure Beach, N Carolina
  60 at Captiva in Florida

Things I like about you... Jane

o Your gentle nature
• your great sense of humor
o the way your eyes twinkle right before you make a joke!
o Your quick smile
• your friendly personality
• How you always find a positive side to every person you encounter and every situation
• that you are so family oriented and have a strong faith
• that you are just plain fun to be around

One friend wrote the following letter which was at the end of the book-
let:

Jane,

I know it is difficult to convey in writing what I mean to tell you, but it
is also impossible sometimes to say the right words, too.

We all know your prognosis is not good, yet we do not rule out the possibility of a long future for you. Not only because of our love for you, but
also because of what we learn from you that gives us hope.

Forgive me if it makes you sadder to deal with what seems to be "what
people always say." I do hold that unreasonable hope.

I want to tell you what you have taught me because these are important
things.

You show me how to be determined without being loud or bossy. You
are a quiet person who does not insist that everyone pay attention to you. But
you also do not back off on stating your own beliefs. I see you always willing
to say what you think, even if others don't like it.

That makes me consider my own bravery. Thank you for showing me
how to be brave.

I also like to think about the gentle way you chuckle at the nonsense we
engage in. Because of this, I realize that one doesn't have to be "the life of
the party" to find happiness in little corners. You always find it. I have never
seen you miss a joke & you have a wry sense of humor. You also teach me
about grace. I am always impressed with the dignified grace you show in any
situation. You are filled with grace because you are unfailingly kind. In one
way or another, you always include others without making them feel out of
place. That is no small task. Quiet people often keep to themselves, but you
are not quiet because you are afraid to speak but because you know how to
quietly help others feel a part. This stems from both your bravery and your
humor. People are important to you.

You are an amazing person, Jane. I hope you know that. I repeat what
others have said, "Let us know what you need." You are always in our hearts
and prayers.

Love, Marcia

I later learned that once during this trip Jane was swimming and felt that she had some weakness on her left side and had to get some help getting out of the pool and decided to not go swimming again. Since she was a good swimmer, I imagine that was frightening.

When I picked her up at the airport the following Saturday on the 15th, it looked to me like she had some definite weakness in her left leg. She did not look the same. That evening she was to start taking her last course of the temozolomide oral chemotherapy that is used for primary brain cancers. It was a 5-day regimen, her 6th course of that. This course would originally have been started on the 7th, the day before she left to go to Florida, but we had talked with Dr. Shanks about delaying it till she got back for a variety of safety reasons. She did not want to stay home and miss out on the trip.

She was scheduled to get her 3 months follow up brain MRI on Friday November 21st at Woodwinds and then see Dr. Shanks and Dr. Cameron on the following Tuesday. However, that Friday afternoon, before we left Woodwinds, Dr. Cameron called and talked to us on the phone to let us know that the scan showed clear signs of recurrence of the tumor growth. It was enough that she was concerned and wanted Jane to begin a course of high dose dexamethasone- steroid- to reduce brain swelling. We got the medication within an hour or two from the Walgreens pharmacy in Cottage Grove.

While in Florida, one of her group had had a significant cough. After getting home, many of the gals ended up getting bronchitis. Jane started to cough sometime that week and have cold symptoms. The following evening on Saturday Jane suddenly became weak enough up in our bedroom that she slumped to the floor and could not get up by herself and I could not get her up. I called the paramedics, and Jane was taken to St. Joseph's hospital. Even after I called the paramedics, she was telling me that she was ok and did not need to go to the hospital. Her severe left sided weakness told me otherwise.

After her first surgery in March, it had been a miracle that she was entirely normal neurologically- no trouble with her strength or thinking or speech etc. This night when she was admitted to the hospital, she had severe paralysis on the left side of her body. I remember being so scared. I did go home to sleep that night and Sarah stayed with her at the hospital. I remember waking up early and talking to Jane's nurse just before the shift change at 7 a.m. She said that Jane had actually got up to the bathroom with help earlier in the night! What a miracle! The steroids had reduced swelling and her strength had improved enough that she could walk!

The medical team determined that it would be her best option to have another surgery both to biopsy and remove the growth. She needed to have an IVC (inferior vena cava) filter placed because she would need to be off the blood thinner for the surgery and afterwards for a while. She also had to have a functional MRI to help plan the surgery. A functional MRI helps to determine exactly what parts of the brain perform various functions for that person. On that Tuesday November 25th, she was found to have pneumonia and was put on antibiotic. She had had enough of being in the hospital and wanted to go home.

She was discharged that Wednesday- the day before Thanksgiving. Our children made the meal- all of them chipped in to make the usual Thanksgiving meal that Jane would normally make mostly on her own. We had roasted turkey, sweet potatoes with brown sugar and pecans, mashed potatoes, cranberry salad, buns, and pecan and pumpkin pies among other dishes. But Jane seemed worse to me on that Thanksgiving Thursday and I wondered if she had come home too soon. Each day I was listening to her lungs to see if they were clearing.

She was tentatively scheduled for surgery on the Tuesday after Thanksgiving- December 2nd. Each day over the weekend I was listening to her lungs- and continuing to hear the sounds of pneumonia at the base on the one side. If her pneumonia did not clear, she would not be able to go ahead with surgery. But the longer they delayed, the more the risk for further growth of her tumor.

On that Sunday, two days before her surgery, her lungs sounded clear! Hallelujah! It was looking like she would be able to go ahead with her surgery.

That Tuesday her surgery was done by Dr. Gregory and Dr. Mary Dunn. We had been told beforehand that without surgery she might only have a month to live due to the size of the tumor and the swelling. With the surgery, she might have 3-6 months. It could be longer, but they could not promise anything. Jane wanted to be alive for the children. She was not ready to die.

After the surgery, Dr. Gregory told us that the pathologist had said it was definite recurrence and that he and Dr. Dunn had tried to be as careful as possible to take as much as possible to give her more time to live, but to not cause any more trouble than necessary. He said that when she was woken after the surgery, she was not able to move her left side. He thought she would regain some function, but time would tell how much.

It was hard for me to see her completely paralyzed on the left side again after the surgery after the improvement she had had from the effect of the steroids earlier. The following entry from my diary gives you more of a feeling of what it was like.

December 4, 2014   Am I Going Down the Tubes?

Last night when I was with Jane at the hospital, she had had a difficult day. She has a dense left hemiparesis, weakness on the left side of the face, and a very junky cough and difficulty bringing up any of that sputum. I had asked the nurse (Donna) if anyone had listened to her lungs, and she asked if I wanted to listen and gave me her stethoscope. Her left side sounded clear (where the pneumonia had been last week). But the right-side base sounded dull and a few rales there. I was fearing she could have either aspiration pneumonia or just a pneumonia from her weakness and preop bronchitis leaving her with residual inflammation etc.

I asked to see which doctors had seen her during the day and Donna saw notes from Dr Hungs and Dr Cameron and I think the speech therapist. But no hospitalist note. Jane had been downgraded from ICU to telemetry on Wednesday afternoon by Dr. Reilkoff, but no hospitalist had seen her for overall coordination and review of the basic issues (that is, for over 24 hours). So of course, I became upset and requested a hospitalist see her and evaluate her lungs etc. Fortunately, Dr. Maddali was on and she had admitted Jane on the evening of 11/22 and so knew her case. She ordered a CXR and lab work but did not come to see her for several hours till that had been done and results were available. I know Jane was stable, but I was irritated that she did not come and see her and evaluate her first. I had not met Dr. Maddali, but when she came in, she did her job, addressed both my concerns and Jane's concerns, made sure she got our questions answered. She felt Jane was fluid overloaded and was going to change her IV fluid amounts and give her some furosemide which is a diuretic.

So, I was definitely doing the physician part above with those details. It was when her lab came back, and her hemoglobin was down to 10.8 and her platelets were 104,000 (normal about 140,000-400,000), that I became additionally worried. Jane could see that in my face. She asked me "Am I going down the tubes?" Her voice was raspy, her face looked puffy and the right side of her face was bruised- from having the right-sided craniotomy.

I hope and pray so much that she can have some significant improvement here today. It would help her spirits- she is fighting hard, but I cannot imagine how difficult it would be to endure all this. May God give her the strength to get better. She is not ready to die, and I do not believe it is her time yet.

After the treatment that Dr. Maddali ordered, Jane did start doing better over that night and the next day. She got physical therapy every day. I could not see how she was going to be able to come straight home. Her left leg and arm were so weak that they provided no support. The physical therapist had her start using a hemi walker which you hold on your good side when you have weight on your bad leg. The therapist was right there with her to make sure she did not fall. She was determined that she did not want to go to a transitional care unit (TCU). On Sunday December 7th, I had visited two different TCUs- one in St. Paul and one in West St. Paul. They both looked nice. I thought that having Jane go to the TCU would be best so that she could have daily or twice daily PT. But she would not consider that- she was determined to go home.

So, on that Monday December 8th, she was transported home by HealthEast Medivan since she was wheelchair bound and I could not transfer her into and out of the wheelchair and we had no ramps into the house.

There was a little ice on the front sidewalk from Sunday's precipitation, but it worked fine for the Medivan attendant to wheel Jane to the front steps. She then had Jane stand and walk with our assistance into the house going up the step to the porch and then the step into the house. Then Jane did walk with the hemi walker with our assistance to the hospital bed in the family room. She was home!

Chapter Fourteen

HOME AGAIN

Jane stayed on the main floor of our home since she could not safely go up the stairs to our bedroom. The hospital bed in the family room was situated so that she could see the tv. We quickly learned how to best do a sponge bath each morning in the bed, since we had no shower or bath on the main floor. Even if we had one there, she was not initially strong enough to do that safely by herself.

With me or someone else by her side, she was able to walk from the bed to the kitchen- there is a step between the family room and kitchen. Physical therapy taught her to step up first with the good leg, and to go down first with the bad leg. With the strength that you need going up and down steps, that maximizes your control and safety in doing the step.

That week the home care nurse started coming as well as the physical therapist and then the occupational therapist. Each day Jane was getting stronger in the left leg. She was never able to really use her left hand again, but her leg strength improved so that she did not have to use the hemi walker on a regular basis. We were both so thankful that she retained the use of her right hand since she was right-handed. That was so helpful for her basic functioning.

It was a joyous day when Jane was able to walk up the stairs to get to our bedroom once again. That month of December 2014, we had the remodeling of our master bathroom mostly finished. Jane had decided on a soft pale-yellow color for the paint on the wall. The toilet was an elevated seat so that it was easier for Jane to use. In early January, the glass surrounding our new shower was installed and Jane was able to sit on a shower chair to take her shower and I would help her dry off afterwards. On the walls in the bathroom, we had placed two watercolor prints that we had purchased from up north. One was Morning Glow and the other Arrowhead Evening- both by Russell Norberg. Both gave such a peaceful feeling to that space.

After healing from the brain surgery in December, the recommendation from Drs. Shanks and Cameron was that Jane should start a type of chemotherapy called Avastin (bevacizumab) that was usually tolerated well and had shown some benefit in cases such as hers. Because of the difficulty starting IVs with her small veins and the need for multiple IV treatments, Jane was scheduled to have a "port" put in on January 9, 2015. Dr. Hartigan placed this at St. John's hospital.

The port was placed in the right upper part of her chest. Anytime she needed blood drawn, or any intravenous treatment done, the port could be accessed. She would not have to have multiple needlesticks for those things. Even though a port can have its own risks, certainly for Jane the benefits far outweighed any risks. She had her first Avastin treatment on January 20th and then every 2 weeks.

From my diary on January 13th, 2015- "Hurray!"

Tonight, Tom and Darcy came over after supper. At first Tom had said they would be here for supper, then later called and said they would be here about 6:30 or 6:45. When they had not come by 7:20, I called as Jane asked me to call him. They were at the round-about on Jamaica avenue and stopped and got Subway sandwiches for dinner.

When they got to the house and settled in, they shared the good news that Darcy was pregnant! Jane was so excited. She has been looking forward to having a grandchild for such a long time. She cried and we all hugged. Darcy is about 10 weeks along and is seeing a midwife at Park Nicollet clinic and they had been able to hear the fetal heart rate today at their visit this afternoon. She had had a positive pregnancy test on Thanksgiving Day and had known when they came over to our house but had not wanted to share given how early it was, etc.

It was a wonderful gift of good news to hear today!

Another diary entry-

I am writing this on the 18th (February 18, 2015). Last Friday, as every day, seems to fly by. We had Rolf Olson over for supper and Jane and I and Rolf talked about her questions about heaven and his understanding (Rolf is a pastor at a Lutheran church in the ELCA). It did help her to think of heaven as a state where we exist with a different energy level, or a different form of energy than here on earth. She feels the "Sunday School" version of heaven is not real.

After Rolf had left and when we were getting ready for bed, Jane said that she wanted me to feel free to meet someone else after she died and not live my life alone. That is awfully hard for me to think about. I don't think I can ever love someone that way that I have loved Jane since I met her in early 1973. She has fulfilled my life in so many ways.

She has taught me so much about life, about love, about family, and about living.

Right now, it is just so difficult to see her not feeling well and not being able to do what she used to do.

I will have to think about this and write more later. Now is not the time.

On February 22, 2015, Jane sent me an e-mail with the subject "Charities, funeral, update". She had listed what songs she wanted sung at her funeral, who she wanted to sing, what hymns she wanted to use, etc. and a statement about what she had learned in life. She did not want to talk about it, she did not want to die, she wanted to just live and make the best of every day, but she planned for that time.

Another entry in my diary on February 24, 2015-

Jane worried about me being alone.

"Last night as we were going to bed, Jane had a difficult moment and was feeling angry that she got this cancer, frustrated, and down. She said she did not want me to come home to an empty house after work. She did not want me to be alone in bed at night. I told her that we will always be together- I will never leave her and she will never leave me. Our spirits will find a way to be together no matter what happens. I must trust God that this will be the case. So many times, I have heard other men be frustrated with their wives and not be happy about various aspects of their relationships. I know that I have been blessed with the most wonderful woman in the world to be my wife and I am thankful for the over 40 years that we have had together. And I am thankful for whatever time that we have remaining. I too have my down times, get angry at God, can't understand why this is happening, etc. I keep trying to live in the moment. I do not want to get caught up in worrying about the future......."

As I think and write today, I know that our marriage has been wonderful, and we have had so many wonderful times together. But no marriage is perfect. All relationships have their challenges. It is not if you have challenges, but how you handle them that defines your relationship. Also, you cannot control how your partner feels or behaves. That is why some wonderful people do not resolve their differences and end up getting divorced. My father and mother were an example of that situation. But that is another story.

Jane in 1954

Jane's high school senior picture

Jane and I on our wedding day

Jane's college graduation

Jane and I at Sarah and Jake's wedding in 2011

Jane and I with our family

Jane enjoying a hike in Door County, October 2013

Jane with GNO group in November 2014 on Captiva Island, Florida

Chapter Fifteen

UNDERSTANDING EACH OTHER

Jeff to Jane note- not dated- but years before she got her brain cancer—
It is so hard for me to understand your behavior.
You don't have to be home alone so much.
You choose to be home alone.

I feel like I have always been there for you. I continue to work when I did not feel like it so that our family would have the resources we needed to live. I know that I don't know exactly what it is like for you. You are right that you don't know what it is like for me. When I see someone almost die or be given a diagnosis of a terminal cancer- both happened this week- I feel like I want to be with you more and hug you and know that you want to hug me. Last night I just wanted to hug you. I am just sad that you sincerely do not want me to be close to you. If I were a dog, you would pet me more than you touch me. I understand you are tired of years of cooking and cleaning and raising children and doing things for me.

You do not have to clean for me or cook for me etc. I can get my own dinner tonight. I can clean the house. But I don't know if I can live without your wanting to touch me. I can only believe you are angry at me when you don't want to touch me. That is why I said I almost wished you would hit me or yell at me. At least I would have contact with you.

Do not feel like you have to do anything for me today. Please take care of yourself.

I pray that God will touch you with his loving hands and heal you.

I pray that God will give me the patience to wait and the wisdom to know how to help. I can't stand to see the wonderful woman I have known these years appear to feel like she wants to shut me out of her life. That is the message your body language tells me despite what you write in your note.

I do love you and always will.

Jane note to Jeff- not dated- but in response to the earlier note---

It's so hard for me to understand your behavior. You know I have not been feeling the best and you still blame me and get mad at me.

I feel like I have always been there for you. I am always here for you and always home when you come home. Maybe I don't know what your work life is like, but you don't have any idea what it is like for me and has been like for me all these years when you are gone so much. I wonder what things would be like if I were the one gone all the time.

Right now, life is just not exciting for me when I have to be home alone so much. It is hard for me to be excited about anything right now. I am trying to find different ways of keeping busy and finding some fun in life like reading or sewing.

If you want me to be closer to you then I need you to be understanding and not accusing and angry.

I need you to understand that I may not be meeting your needs right now but I know I will be fine and find my place and our relationship can get back on track.

You need to trust me. I know you need hugs right now. I get it. I just need to take care of myself for a while.

I am writing this out so you can look at it whenever you feel like you do now. I don't know how many more times I can explain this.

I love you and always will.

Asking for Forgiveness

We all make mistakes in life. No one is perfect. At least I have not run into anyone who is perfect. Jane was the closest, but she was not perfect either.

When we would have our squabbles, I was usually the one in the wrong. I just could not see it immediately.

Many times, I asked for her forgiveness.

In 2009, the Great Recession had hit many people hard. Many lost their jobs, as well as their homes, to this event. In the summer of 2009, a bill called the CARS Act (Consumer Assistance to Recycle and Save Act) was passed by the House of Representatives. It was also called "cash for clunkers". It ended up being rolled into the Supplemental Appropriations Act, 2009 as Title XIII, and was effective in early July. The purpose was to stimulate the economy by selling more new cars and help the environment by having more cars with better fuel efficiency. There were various criteria such as needing to be in drivable condition, having been registered and insured for a minimum of one year before the trade-in, generally getting less than 18 miles per gallon, and that the new vehicle being bought had to get at least 22 miles per gallon for passenger automobiles.

I wrote Jane the following note on August 1, 2009:

Dear Jane,

I heard that Congress passed a new addition to the CARS (cash for clunkers) program. If your husband has screwed up enough times, then you qualify to trade him in for a new model and you get a sizable tax credit. You qualify if he has been acting as a bonehead, you have been married more than 20 years, and you have put up with multiple occurrences of this problem. I think you qualify for this new program.

You put your husband in the doghouse (I know I'm already in it) and ship him C.O.D. (the government knows you don't want to pay yourself for the shipping) to the nearest rehabilitation center. There are only a few qualified centers in the U.S. If they are not able to process him into a model that is acceptable to you, then you can get a new model – free of charge – under the 2009 Marriage Recovery Act.

Oh, how I know I screwed up – please forgive me. Life when we are separated in mind, spirit, and body is no longer worthwhile.

       Love, Me 😞
       (can become 🙂 with your forgiveness)

Jeff's thoughts-   How is it that sometimes it is so easy to love someone and live with that person and be so happy? How is it that with that same person it can be such a struggle to understand each other and forgive each other? We never know exactly what it is to be another person with those different experiences and those different genetic traits. We never know exactly the entire internal thoughts and feelings that another person has had over their lifetime. We only know our own experience and how our own body feels.

Even with the occasional times such as above, I was so blessed to have known Jane for over 43 years and to be married to her for over 41 years. Her love, her thoughtfulness, her friendship, her companionship, and her joy were such a blessing to me.

Chapter Sixteen

SPRING OF 2015

I am writing on March 12, 2015. Yesterday we saw Dr. Cameron. The brain MRI on March 10th was essentially the same as the one post op in December according to Dr. Cameron. She said that Avastin affects the appearance of the perfusion sequences on the MRI but that other than that, it looked similar to before. So that was good news.

We asked her about the path report from Mayo. Dr. Shanks had said that he would either send the tissue to Mayo or if Jane was in the study, then it would be sent to Michigan for a second opinion from the reading by the St. Joseph's pathologists- Dr. Leverone I think. We understood that both from the neurosurgeons and the interpretation of the path by Dr. Leverone that she had definite tumor recurrence causing the trouble in late November that required the repeat neurosurgery on Dec. 2nd. But the Mayo report stated the tissue was primarily tumor necrosis from the previous therapy and only saw a few quiescent astrocytoma cells. Dr. Shanks had talked to the Mayo pathologist before he saw us on March 3rd. So, Jane had gotten excited that it meant that she had a much better prognosis.

Dr. Cameron explained that when neurosurgery is done, the fragments of tissue are not all prepared to look at under the microscope and she and the neurosurgeons felt that it must have been a sampling issue that led to the Mayo pathologist giving the reading as above. So, after we got home, even though the MRI report was good, Jane was significantly down about the pathology report. Dr. Cameron had told us that on the initial path report a year ago, that Jane did not have any of the 3 tumor markers that can give a more favorable prognosis- IDH1/IDH2 negative, 1p/19q deletion negative, and MGMT gene for motor methylation negative.

Dr. Cameron stated that a year ago when Jane was post op from initial surgery and the MRI showed sign of recurrence already, she was very concerned that Jane would be one of those that only lived 6-9 months and that she had already done better than expected.

She spent a long time talking with us. I explained that I had been concerned because Dr. Shanks had said he would send the path for a 2nd opinion whether or not Jane was in the study, and then did not do so, and when we saw him in February and we asked about it, he asked if we wanted to have him send it to the Mayo clinic. We did ask him to go ahead and send it to Mayo, and then on March 3rd we got the information as above and he gave me a copy of Mayo's report.

After all this, there are times I just do not know what to think. I continue to try to live one day at a time and not worry about what the future will bring. I sure hope that we have done the best that we could. I think that we have. It would be so difficult to travel to a different part of the country for treatment.

Today Jane said that on one of the tv shows there was information that a trial at Duke University had used tetanus booster to make a treatment work better for GBM (glioblastoma multiforme). There are so many times that tv reports gloss over significant issues and make it sound that something is proven to work. As best I could find on the web, including the Duke University site, the study only involved about a dozen people. They were randomized, half given tetanus booster, then all treated with a dendritic cell vaccine. The ones given tetanus booster did significantly better with longer survival times.

March 17, 2015 Chemo Day

Today was a long day at chemotherapy. We left at 8 a.m. Today also was the first day that Kristine and Laura were to clean our house. We thought we would be back before they were done. Our appointment was at 8:30. They wanted Jane to give a urine sample to check for protein and the result had to be known before they would order the chemotherapy (Avastin). She was initially not able to go even though she felt like she had to do so. So, she drank some water and was later able to go. Then there was a delay because the Avastin is not actually ordered until the lab results are back. Dr. Shanks is on vacation this week, so the chemo nurses had to wait for the nurse practitioner to order it and she was in a patient room for a visit. Then after the chemo is ordered, it takes a while for the pharmacy to mix it up. So, it was not until about 11:20 a.m. before the Avastin was going in the IV into Jane's port, and they infuse it over 1 hour since she seems to tolerate it better than when it is infused over 1/2 hour. So, it was about 12:45 p.m. before we left St. John's chemotherapy outpatient infusion center today.

We stopped at Walgreens to pick up some prescriptions and then a treat at Dairy Queen-a snickers Blizzard for Jane and a chocolate mint Blizzard for myself. Coming home, the house smelled of cleaning as we walked in the door and Kristine and Laura had left a note. It looks like they did a good job. With everything else to do, and Jane's physical limitations, it was so helpful to have someone else to do the housecleaning.

Jane and I ultimately decided to pursue a second opinion at the Mayo Clinic regarding the current management of her situation. We saw Dr. Jan Buckner on April 1, 2015 and it was his opinion that the primary difficulty in December of 2014 was due to swelling and necrosis of the tumor from the radiation therapy and since the March 2015 brain MRI did not show any evidence of progression, he felt that it was appropriate to discontinue the Avastin chemotherapy. He recommended having another MRI in 2 months- i.e., in May and said the Avastin could always be restarted. Jane was happy to discontinue the chemotherapy and see what happened.

I made a diary entry on April 4th, 2015---- Face symptoms

"This morning before I went to renewal, Jane was having the pulling sensation in the right cheek that she has had at times. She had felt it in the past when it was thought to be migraine headache aura. She asked Dr. Buckner at Mayo if he saw anything on the scan to explain this, and he said the left side of the brain looked fine. He said other than the area of treatment where she had the two surgeries, radiation, etc., that her brain looked like a young brain. She only had one spot of white matter consistent with ischemic changes and it was very small. She did not have the chronic small vessel ischemic disease that so many people will have at her age.

She also felt her eyes were dry this morning and asked me to put in the lubrication drops that she has.

It is simply hard for her to have these other sensations and wonder if something else is going on. We will just have to see.

Chapter Seventeen

GOLFING

When Jane turned 40, she decided she needed to take up an activity that she could do with friends for enjoyment. She thought about playing cards, but never really enjoyed doing that. She decided to take up golfing. She ended up joining a league of women that golfed from May thru August at Cimarron golf course in Lake Elmo. It was a time to share with friends. She tried to play her best, but it was never to be competitive against other people. It was for the joy of being with friends. She would say that even if you could not play golf well, you could dress to look like you played well. Many of the friends who played in this league were teachers. When they were still working, they would not be able to start playing until school was done. When they retired, they were able to start playing in early to mid-May and then by the middle part of August they would have their banquet after their final weekly round, so that the teachers still working would be able to return to their jobs.

We went to the Brainerd Lakes area for a vacation week many times in the summer and we would play golf at the 9-hole course at Grand View Lodge. Jane always loved the beauty of the pine and oak trees, and the wildlife that we would see- whether it would be an eagle, loons flying over, various songbirds, or at different times an army of dragonflies in perfect formation. The flowers were always beautiful at the tee boxes and other areas of the course. I have so many wonderful memories of times we shared together with smiles and laughter.

When she had her surgery in December of 2014 and was paralyzed on the left side, it was not too long after that she said we were going to return to Grand View that next summer and she was going to play golf there again. It was hard to see how this was going to occur. But when she put her mind to it, I knew that I should not doubt that.

She fulfilled that goal in July of 2015(almost 40 years after we were married and had spent our honeymoon at Grand View) when we stayed at our quarter share on Middle Cullen lake and we went to the Grand View course. Jane did not play the entire 9 holes, but she played as many holes as she could- holding the golf club with mostly her right hand, hitting some wonderful shots straight down the fairway. She and Sarah rode the cart together as they often had- mother and daughter enjoying their time together.

Chapter Eighteen

FIRST GRANDCHILD!

August 2015

Tom called about 7:30 this morning saying that Darcy had delivered at 5:42 a.m.

Jane and I got up and got ready. It was a little after 10 a.m. when we were ready to leave to go to the hospital. Tom told us to take I-494 to Hwy 169 north and then take Excelsior Blvd east to Methodist hospital, since Hwy 100 was partly closed.

When we got there, Chris and Julie were already there.

The baby's name is Ruby Jane Nelson- they only told us that after we got to the hospital. She was 8 # 9 oz., 22 inches long, and head circumference 13 1/2 ". Of course, as a family physician who had previously delivered babies, I had to ask the labor nurse what Ruby's Apgar scores were. They were 7 & 9 which is very normal.

Darcy had some contractions start last evening and yesterday was her due date. They went to the hospital about 2 a.m. She was having enough pain that she decided she wanted to have an epidural and the nurse checked her, and she was nearly complete, so they held off on the epidural and she delivered without that.

We got to hold Ruby Jane- the first time I held her she definitely looked right at me and right at Jane. It is not common for a newborn baby to have such a definite focus on your face as Ruby had. She later closed her eyes and was sleeping.

Darcy was first in a labor room where she delivered, and it was not long after we got there that the nurses moved her to another room. I had gone to Cub as Jane requested to get some flowers and donut holes. I saw a dozen peach roses that looked nice and the staff person- Sharon- was so helpful- she arranged the flowers in a glass quart jar that was painted pink. I got both regular cake donut holes and blueberry flavored ones.

After Darcy moved to her new room, Sarah and Jake came, and they brought an assortment of donuts with them! So, we had plenty of treats!

It was a blessing that Darcy's labor and delivery were relatively easy, and that Ruby Jane was doing fine.

We got pictures of Ruby and Tom and Darcy as well as Ruby being held by Jane and Sarah. Darcy's parents Mariann and Wayne came also. Then we left about 1PM or so as we thought Darcy needed to be able to get some rest. Sarah and Jake apparently left about 20 minutes after we did.

We went home and Jane took a nap. Jane and I visited Chris and Julie later about 5:30 p.m. to see Julie's sister Katie and her family who had been visiting them since Wednesday night. Then we went back to the hospital to visit Tom & Darcy and Ruby for another hour or so.

All in all, it was a special day.
Jane has looked forward to having grandchildren for some time.

Chapter Nineteen

RECURRENCE

August 19, 2015

Today Jane and I went down to the Rochester Mayo clinic for her MRI brain scan and later consult with Dr. Buckner this afternoon. At Mayo, their safety protocol for infusing thru the port required them to have information I was not expecting. One piece was verification of the tip of the catheter. So, I called St. Joseph's radiology and had them fax the report by Dr. Hartigan of 1-9-2015 where he used fluoroscopy for placement of the port to prove the tip was at the cavo-atrial junction. Even though Jane had had multiple MRIs with contrast since the port had been placed, that was not acceptable to Mayo. It took the staff at Mayo a long time to come up with a fax number that the report could be faxed to. The nurse was very nice but seemed to be fairly new with how she handled things with Jane which at first was making her uncomfortable. So, despite the long wait and the hassle involved, it all worked out and the scan was done.

We had lunch at the Mayo cafeteria which is on the subway level just east of the Gonda and Mayo buildings and talked with one couple from Quincy, Illinois. The husband had Lewy body dementia and his wife was seeing ophthalmology for her glaucoma. Then an elderly lady from St. Paul and a man from Austin, Minnesota next sat at our group of tables before we finished our lunch. We talked about how Donald Trump would make a poor president with the way he had so far handled himself in his candidacy and the first Republican debate.

We saw Dr. Buckner in the afternoon and the news was not good. The scan showed definite progression of tumor growth. Dr. Buckner said he was 95% certain that it was cancer and not treatment effect and he definitely recommended that we do some form of treatment and not just observe.

He said he thought Jane qualified for a study involving surgery to remove the mass and injecting measles virus around the surgical site. But the neurosurgeon was not available to talk to us that afternoon. He also said she might qualify for proton beam radiation and he would have the radiation oncologist at Mayo review her scans and case. He said he would try to have them get back to us later this week. The other options include resuming Avastin, with or without radiation therapy. Everything is basically experimental because there is no proven therapy for this situation.

Jane trusted Dr. Vogel and Dr. Cameron the most on her team of physicians. So given this issue, I paged Dr. Cameron when we got home. She was able to call us right back and we talked for about half an hour. Her radiation oncology residency was at Massachusetts General Hospital (MGH) in Boston. MGH was the second center in the United States to use proton beam therapy and the first to use it primarily for clinical studies. She said there was no proven benefit to that versus standard radiation therapy regarding side effects. Theoretically proton beam therapy can be adjusted to minimize radiation to surrounding tissue to reduce the cognitive side effects, but she said this was not shown to be the case in adults, but that in children it was shown to help.

Jane's case will be presented at the HealthEast neurologic tumor conference on Monday morning, the 24th. Then we will see Dr. Cameron the following morning.

Dr. Buckner did recommend keeping her steroid at the current dose- he did not think it needed to be increased at this time since he did not see any brain swelling. He did not think the urinary tract infections and tailbone pain were related to the recurrent brain tumor. Jane had had 6 episodes of urinary tract infections that were caused by the bacteria Klebsiella pneumonia on 5 of those 6 occasions in the last 3 months.

He did think her episodes of metallic taste in the mouth were minor seizures but since they were brief and not connected with other symptoms, he advised we keep seizure meds the same for now.

August 21, 2015 Journey into Space

Late this afternoon Jane decided she wanted to go see the show at the Omni theater before it was done on Sunday. We did not have time to eat before getting to the 6 p.m. show, so we had some crackers in the car on the way to the Science Museum. We drove on Warner road to the Science Museum parking lot, and parked on level P2, and took the elevator up to the lobby level. We went outside on the veranda around the tugboat exhibit- the afternoon was beautiful, and it felt good to be outside. We looked at the cross section of the white pine tree from Itasca State Park that lived from about 1703 until 1999 when it came down- around 296 years! Then I thought we just needed to go up to the top floor for the entrance that avoided all the stairs, but Jane thought we needed to have our tickets scanned- and she was right.

After scanning the tickets, then we took the elevator to get to the 6th floor level. We went around to the left side because that side had the women's bathroom- she had felt her stomach was uncertain. We sat in the "reserved" seats which did not require going up or down any stairs- we were able to sit in the ones most toward the center of the theater and so had particularly good seats.

There was a preview of a Humpback whale show that is coming next- some beautiful footage of humpback whales and the ocean. The Journey into Space show had footage from several other shows as well as computer animation as well as including pictures from the Hubble telescope. It is about the plan to eventually travel to Mars. The beauty of the universe, the hope for the future, the desire by man to explore--- all of it was so uplifting. Jane really enjoyed it and felt it was the best Omni theater show that she had seen.

After the show we went to the Science Museum shop- I usually do not get anything. Jane was looking to see what they had in t-shirts. They did have one for infants that was so cute. It had Ba B Y on the front with the letters of the 3 elements- Barium, Boron, and Yttrium to reflect the Table of Elements. We got one for Chris and Julie's baby that is due in February. Then Jane found one for me that says, "May the forest be with you" to paraphrase the term "May the force be with you" from the Star Wars Trilogy movies. Lastly, I saw a DVD of the Hubble telescope Omni theater show that I wanted to get.

We stopped at Culver's and had a cheeseburger for supper on our way home. Then we came home and took a walk on the street out to 90th- just part way to the farmhouse because she was tired- and back.

All in all, it was a beautiful evening together.

Earlier in the day I had picked up the CD of her brain MRI scan from Wednesday at Mayo that had been overnight expressed to Dr. Vogel and took it to Woodwinds to be entered in the HealthEast PACS (Picture Archival System). If the regular courier system had done this, it would have taken too long. Her case will be presented Monday morning at the tumor conference per Dr. Cameron. Then we see her Tuesday morning to get her thoughts.

After stopping at Woodwinds, I then went to the St. Paul Eye clinic in Stillwater to see Dr. Kennedy regarding my right eye that has had persisting redness and developed swelling of the infero-medial sclera. She said it was not anything serious, "chemosis" and gave me Alrex- an intermediate potency steroid to use 4 x per day for 5 days as well as a moisturizer "Blink".

I stopped at Bonngard's Meat shop as Jane asked me to do to get a roast beef sandwich that we split for lunch. Then while she took a nap, I got some work done on the computer. Since we did not hear from Mayo, I called in the early afternoon to Dr. Buckner's secretary, Sue Stotzheim, and then in the later afternoon to Butch Kvittem who does coordination for their research program. We had seen her on Wednesday after Dr. Buckner's visit. Sue called back right after my call to Butch- too soon for her to have had a chance to do anything- with the appointment for Sept 2 to see Dr. Parney. Since I wondered if that was timely enough given the scan results, she will check with Dr. Buckner on Monday when he is back. She said he was gone the last two days. Apparently, Dr. Parney is also gone until the week of August 31st. I asked Sue if they could e-mail the research protocol on the possible trial that Jane may participate in. We wanted to get whatever information was available to consider that option. She was able to do that.

August 25, 2015

Today we went to see Dr. Cameron for an early morning appointment. Unfortunately, the MRI of the brain from Mayo of August 19,2015 when loaded onto the HealthEast PACS does not load correctly and just gives error messages. I stopped in radiology after the appointment with Dr. Cameron at Woodwinds, and the tech there showed me that it was copied onto the system and there are 3500+ images there and so it is a very large file, but when I talked to Dr. Veldman at Woodwinds over the phone and later Dr. Blake Carlson who was at the HealthEast Imaging Center(he had read some of Jane's earlier scans)- they could not get the images to load to be able to look at them even though it looks like they are on the system. Dr. Carlson had me call St. Paul Radiology and talked to the tech there. She could see the file quickly, but the images would not load, so she said the disc had to be corrupted in some fashion and recommended we have Mayo send a new disc.

I called Sue Steinmetz at Mayo and she had a new copy sent.

When we talked with Dr. Cameron, we spent about 40 minutes with her. She said there is no way to tell the best option and that Jane needs to go with what her heart tells her or what she feels God tells her thru prayers. Her case had been presented at tumor conference, but they did not have the MRI images to look at due to above problem. She said that one option is to use Cyberknife since the cavity had shrunk from earlier in the year and in general, depending on the location in the brain, if tumor is smaller than 5 cm then the Cyberknife can be used. (She said there were a lot of other details that decided what size it could be used for). That would involve 10 fractions of radiation done every other day- Monday, Wednesday, Friday for 3 weeks with one more treatment. Another option is to use the Avastin with the radiation therapy as long as Jane tolerates it. Another is to have Dr. Gregory do a resection of the recurrent tumor and apparently HealthEast is participating in a study that has to do with a vaccine that is developed from the tissue of your own tumor. I was unsure if anyone else has had this done at HealthEast. It was a National Institute of Health (NIH) study, multicenter, and it required that there be 7.5 gm of tumor tissue available to make the vaccine. She said we could see Dr. Gregory for a consult regarding any aspect of this.

Then I talked with Sue Steinmetz at Mayo this morning also about their study. Of the 13 patients that have participated since 2006, 4 patients are still alive, and all have been treated within the last 6 months. All but 2 of them have had GBM. I asked if we could get more info regarding the 13 patients- i.e., length of life for each patient etc. She said she had to ask Dr. Buckner and if he could authorize it, then their statistician group would need to prepare a report. When I asked, she did say that one patient had died of complications of surgery about a month or so after the procedure.

August 28, 2015

Jane and I went up to the cabin this weekend. Chris, Tom & Darcy and Ruby, and Sarah and Jake were all able to be there. Jane and I got to "babysit" Ruby for about 2 hours while the rest went to Nisswa for lunch etc. I videotaped Ruby and Jane singing to her as well as took some pictures, as well as hold her myself. Sarah and Jane and I stayed Sunday night while the others had to get back for work etc. We dropped off Sarah at their place today and saw Oskar their dog before going on home.

Jane wanted me to call Dr. Cameron's office as well as Dr. Gregory's. Kathy Meier from Dr. Gregory's office called back and was at the neuro tumor conference on August 24th. She will ask Dr. Gregory what his personal recommendation would be and get back to us in the next day or two. She was going to ask him today, but he had to leave clinic abruptly for an emergency neurosurgery. Since his only office day is Monday and he is booked up for the next several weeks, she will see if it is ok to just schedule surgery if Jane wants to pursue that option with him and whether we could just talk over phone beforehand if Jane needed to do that. Our appointment at Mayo on September 2nd with Dr. Parney was changed to 3:00 p.m. from 4:15 p.m. - We had a message on the answering machine from Mayo when we got home. It is not a big change, but it will be nice to be driving home sooner than it would have been.

Dr. Cameron called back about 7:30 p.m. just as we were returning from a walk.

We needed a few more specifics as best she could tell. We had talked with her for 40 minutes last Tuesday 8/25 but had not covered these specifics. She expected that without any treatment that Jane would probably live about 4 months- sometime around the holidays. She had understood that Jane did not want to have any further surgery and that after reviewing the scan from Mayo, that she was a candidate for the Cyberknife type of radiation therapy. She was not sure that would prolong her life, but the tumor had been radiosensitive in the spring of 2014 and could respond again. It would be likely to cause tiredness for her. It would be an option to do Avastin after the Cyberknife, but she would not do both at the same time due to concern for increased side effects. She thought it was worthwhile to get the second opinion at Mayo and see the neurosurgeon on Wednesday there. Jane does not qualify for any clinical trial here at HealthEast. If Dr. Gregory does surgery here to debulk the tumor, Dr. Cameron would recommend radiation therapy following healing from the surgery. Surgery followed by radiation therapy followed by Avastin would certainly be the most aggressive approach.

No one can say what is likely to be the best approach here for her. It is all experimental at this point.

I write this early on the morning of September 1st. Even though I have realized since last year that Jane could die whether from the cancer or the complications, it is so unreal to think that is coming in this time frame. After the surgery last December, I had somewhat prepared myself mentally for her death and then when she had the good scans in March and in May, both of us started thinking that she could be one of the fortunate ones and have some extended time here.

When I talked with Dr. Cameron, I told her that Jane was not ready to die. Even though we have talked openly about the prognosis from the beginning, she is simply not ready to leave this life, leave our children or her granddaughter. I have to trust that God will take care of her. It is so unreal to be facing this. I pray that God will give both of us the strength that we need, the patience that we need, and the wisdom needed to handle the situations that we will face. I need to continue to try to live today and not fear tomorrow. I pray that we can share God's love and mercy that He has for each and every one of us.

We saw Dr. Ian Parney, neurosurgeon, on September 2, 2015 at 3 p.m. for consultation regarding Jane's options. He knew Jane's case well, was thorough in his discussion and examination, and straightforward in his describing Jane's options and his understanding of the risks and benefits of each of those options. Jane had not wanted to have any more surgery, but after this visit, she decided that she had to give it more thought. She ended up deciding to have this further neurosurgery at the Mayo clinic and participate in the modified measles virus instillation protocol as part of the resection of the recurrent tumor.

This was a two-step procedure, and she was scheduled to have the first surgery on Friday September 11th at St. Mary's hospital in Rochester and the second procedure on Tuesday September 15th at the same location with both by Dr. Parney. During the first procedure, he would perform a stereotactic placement of an intratumoral catheter with virus injection. The second procedure involved en bloc removal of the tumor and catheter and further virus injection into the surgical cavity. That sounds straightforward, but like many things in life, it was more challenging. Jane decided to try this because she was certainly hoping to live longer for the children and grandchildren. She also felt that she was being called to help other people that experienced this type of cancer and wanted to participate in this research trial.

Part of the challenge is that Rochester and the Mayo clinic is about a 70-mile drive from our home. When you think of all the miles that people drive, that does not seem long. But when your baseline state is being easily fatigued, it is much more of a challenge. We drove down on Thursday September 10th for multiple preoperative type appointments including her preop clearance visit. I gave her last dose of Lovenox per protocol that morning so there would be no dose for 24 hours before her surgery. With her high risk for recurrence of deep vein thrombosis or pulmonary embolus, it is usual to give that injectable anticoagulant as a bridge when the warfarin medication that she has been on is being held for the surgery. The neurosurgeon wanted a platelet function test to be a part of the blood tests before surgery. But I knew that the Lovenox would not be worn off by the time that blood sample was drawn that afternoon. So, she could not be fully cleared for surgery that afternoon. The plan was to repeat the test the following morning just before surgery.

Jane and I stayed at a hotel in Rochester to help her get more sleep before that surgery on September 11th. That morning we were up early to go to St. Mary's hospital for her to be admitted. We were there by 5:30 a.m. and I wheeled her in a wheelchair to the place where she was admitted. We did not realize there would be such a line, or that it would be the lengthy process that it was. But she was finally taken to the preoperative area, and the nurse took her vital signs and so forth. But somehow there was no order for the blood test to verify that her blood was clotting normally so that it would be safe to proceed. It seemed like it took forever for the nurse to get the test ordered and have the lab tech come to draw the blood, but it was done, and we waited for the result.

I think it was close to an hour and when I asked the nurse about whether the result was back and we looked into it, it was then realized that the wrong test had been ordered. The resident physician who gave the order thought that she needed a routine PT or prothrombin time or INR test. But that was not the case. She needed the platelet function test. So, the correct test was ordered, but unfortunately, they had to come and draw her blood another time! The great Mayo clinic was not showing its best on that morning and so once again she had to wait much longer than usual for her scheduled surgery. The surgery itself was uncomplicated. Her neurologic status seemed the same afterwards and the plan was for her to be discharged the next day on Saturday.

The main issue that Saturday morning was her bladder function. Because of her bladder laceration at her first C-section in 1980, her multiple bladder infections, etc., she was felt to have hypotonic bladder dysfunction. In other words, her bladder did not contract as well as usual. With the effect of anesthesia, and her lessened mobility from the left hemiparesis, I was concerned that she was not urinating like usual. She was up several times during the night to urinate and that was not typical for her. I asked the nurse that Saturday morning to do a postvoid residual to see how she was emptying her bladder. An ultrasound scan of the bladder can very accurately estimate how much urine is still in the bladder after one has voided. Her postvoid residual was 700 cc which is very abnormal.

She still wanted to go home, and because I could catheterize her as needed, they discharged her home on that Saturday. Overnight we kept track of the volume of how much she urinated. The following morning because of our uncertainty of how she was doing, I catheterized her about an hour after she had urinated (it took a while given her mobility, etc.) and the result was 150 cc. So at least she was doing much better. But an elevated postvoid residual is still one of the reasons that it can be much easier to get a bladder infection.

As a part of the research protocol, we had to drive back to Rochester on Sunday September 13th to have various lab tests drawn. Although we knew the address of the lab, it was a research lab and entrance on a Sunday was not clear, so it took longer than we anticipated. But once there, the blood was drawn, and we drove home.

We returned the following day and stayed overnight at the hotel for the early morning admission on Tuesday the 15th for the main surgical procedure. Fortunately, postoperatively there was no significant difference in her neurologic function after the resection of the area of tumor progression. But she again had trouble with urination and on the evening of the 16th, her scanned postvoid residual was 700 cc. It took several hours before a urologic tech came and did catheterization and she agreed that it was too long from the time the problem had been identified.

Jane was discharged home on Friday the 18th and in the evening, she developed her typical symptoms of bladder infection with pain and feeling lousy. We got a clean catch sample and Dr. Vogel ordered a urinalysis and urine culture and I took the sample to Woodwinds hospital to be processed. Because she was not on warfarin in the immediate postoperative period, she could take ciprofloxacin to clear this infection and the culture confirmed it was susceptible.

Jane was healing from that surgery and doing relatively well, when on Monday October 5th, Sarah paged me at the clinic at 8:38 a.m. to tell me that Jane had lost consciousness and apparently fell off the chair she was sitting on when Sarah was upstairs only briefly to take a shower. I immediately came home, and because of the pain that Jane had in her shoulder and the left side of her neck, I did not think we could safely try to transport her by ourselves to the ER to be seen.

We called the paramedics, and she was transported to Woodwinds hospital emergency room where the various x-rays and CTs showed that she had a left clavicle fracture as well as left second rib fracture. She also had left third and fourth rib fractures that looked to be chronic but new since the studies of March 2014, but there was not anytime that she had injury between 2014 and now that would have explained the 3rd and 4th rib fractures. So, either it was from her initial fall on March 4, 2014 or from the fall today. In either event, this episode and the resulting injuries really set Jane back.

On October 16th, 11 days later, Jane and I were watching a show on PBS, one of her favorite channels. She blurted out, "I don't want to be me anymore." She was so frustrated with her limitations and watching the actors and actresses, she just said she did not want to be herself anymore. She was crying her heart out and with the clavicle and rib fractures, crying hurt a lot. We do not know if her fall was from a syncopal episode or a seizure, but it did not matter. Either way, it really set her back.

Chapter Twenty

CHRISTMAS LETTER AND HOLIDAY EVENTS OF 2015

"Someday the sun will come your way."
—Charlie Brown

December 2015

Let's start with the good news. We were blessed with the arrival of our first grandchild, Ruby Jane, daughter of Tom and Darcy, in August. Chris and Julie are expecting the birth of their first child, a son, in February. What a blessing are both of these events. Sarah and Jake moved into their new home in Minneapolis in June and enjoy their neighborhood.

Jeff's dad turned 90 last July but Jane was not able to travel to see him when his birthday celebration was held. Jane's dad turns 90 in early January and a celebration is planned after Christmas. This last year has been a challenge. Even though Jane's cancer appeared to be in remission last spring, a variety of pains and infections affected most of her days. In August, it was definite that her cancer was growing quickly, and she opted to try an experimental treatment at the Mayo Clinic in September that involved surgery (her

3rd and 4th brain surgeries) and instillation of measles virus. It was going relatively well until a passing out spell caused multiple fractures of the ribs and collar bone that were very painful for much of October. But soon she returned to taking a daily walk down our street to work toward getting her strength back and doing exercises from her therapists. What a beautiful fall and early winter we have had- so many good days for a walk.

We pray for good days for everyone in our family and for all of you in this coming New Year. We thank God for the good days this last year and for the strength to handle the challenging days.

Jane's mantra-
"Live every day like it will be one of the best of days and not the worst of days."

On Monday December 28, 2015, Jane and her sister were planning a celebration for her father's 90th birthday. His actual birthday is in January, but that day worked best for the family members who had to travel a distance. It was scheduled at a restaurant in Burnsville where her parents lived. Jane and I had tried to think of possible options for a gift for Walt. He was a difficult one for whom to buy a birthday present. We thought of a different idea......

From: Jeff Nelson
Sent: 18. December 2015 14:49
To: Norwegian Honorary Consulate General in Minneapolis
Subject: Recognition of a 90-year-old man who has always been a wonderful supporter of Norway

Dear Hon. Consul General Heiberg, or Vice Consul Carleton or Ardakani,

I am writing to ask if it is possible for you to recognize a man for his lifelong commitment to the country of Norway. A simple letter of acknowledgement and thanks to him from one of you would mean the world to him. His family is celebrating his upcoming 90th birthday a little early because that is when the family members- including children, grandchildren, and great-grandchildren- can be in the Twin Cities.

My father-in-law- Walter Eugene Korsrud (date of birth January 8, 1926 - he was born in Glenville Minnesota at home) - has always been such a wonderful "ambassador" for Norway with his traditions and teaching his children and grandchildren as well as friends about the wonderful country of Norway and being Norwegian.

His father was Albert Clarence Korsrud who was a pastor at several Lutheran churches in southern Minnesota- Glenville and the surrounding area.

Walter attended Luther College in Decorah, IA and was successful in having all 3 of his children attend and graduate from Luther- Sandra, David, and Jane. Jane became my wife in 1975 and she was diagnosed with high grade malignant brain cancer in March of 2014 and has had 4 brain surgeries and is currently restarting chemotherapy for apparent recurrence- we have learned to make the most of each day and live life to the fullest.

Walter and Helen Korsrud live at 115 E. Burnsville Parkway, Burnsville, MN 55337. Helen just had a fall and has a pelvic fracture and is at rehab in a transitional care unit not far from where they live.

Walter graduated from high school in Albert Lea in 1943. Between 1944-1946, he served in the U.S. Army, including Nancy, France, and in Germany as an x-ray tech. He graduated from Luther in 1949. He and Helen married at St. Olaf church in Austin, Minnesota on Sept 4, 1948. He worked as a teacher in the Pipestone, Minnesota school system and subsequently as a counselor in the Penn junior high school in Bloomington. He and Helen currently attend Prince of Peace Lutheran Church in Burnsville.

The first Christmas that I spent with Jane and her family in Burnsville was in the mid-1970s and Walt and Helen always upheld the Scandinavian traditions.

They served lutefisk and lefse, etc. Even though my heritage was all Swedish, Walter tolerated me and even made me feel comfortable.

He always says that all babies speak Norwegian before they learn any other language. He taught our three children the Norwegian traditions and taught them how to fish. Whenever he meets someone new, he tells them that he will make them an "honorary" Norwegian if they happen to be of a different heritage.

He has been a faithful provider for his family, lived frugally to be able to pay for his children's college education, and always encourages his family members to get as much education as they can. He has given some support to his grandchildren for their post- high school education.

His father's family was from the area around Lillehammer- Ruddbygd is I think the name of the town. His last name Korsrud, I understand means crossroad in Norwegian.

I understand the family farm in Norway is by a crossroad. On his mother's side of the family, they were from Davik, Norway. He has given me pictures of some of the places in Norway that he was able to visit when he was younger. He paid for my wife and her sister to go on a trip to Norway. Then my brother-in-law and I also went and paid for ourselves. It was a very memorable trip including seeing some relatives in Norway in 1992. I could go on, but I think this is enough detail.

At this point, he did not really want anything physical for his birthday- but we know he will really appreciate the time and effort of his family members to be seeing him soon.

If it meets the approval of your consulate, it would be a wonderful gift from you to have a simple letter of thanks for his support of the country of Norway and its traditions.

Please let me know if you have any questions. If for any reason the above is not possible, if there are any alternatives, please let me know.

Sincerely,
Jeffrey D. Nelson

The Norwegian consulate kindly responded with the following card:

ROYAL NORWEGIAN CONSULATE GENERAL

Dear   Walter Eugene Korsrud,

The Royal Norwegian Honorary Consulate General in Minneapolis would like to congratulate you on your 90th birthday, January 8th 2016.

We would like to commend you for your lifelong commitment to Norway, for being an "Ambassador" for Norway and keeping Norwegian traditions going by teaching your children and grandchildren as well as friends about the wonderful country of Norway and being Norwegian.

Thank you, and Congratulations on your 90th birthday!

With Regards,

Eivind Heiberg
Honorary Consul General

The last Sunday in December we were able to celebrate the baptism of Ruby Jane. Tom and Darcy had her baptized at Wooddale Lutheran where they had been married in 2014. It was fun to celebrate after the ceremony at the church hall with Darcy's family as well as ours.

The next day I was heading out to do an errand and I opened the garage door for the Honda CRV. Suddenly, there was a loud sound and something in the opener broke. It was not the main spring, thankfully, but the opener did not work, and I could not manually get the garage door open. If we were not able to get it fixed, I would not be able to take Jane to her father's 90th birthday celebration in Burnsville! She was unable to get into our Toyota Corolla because it was much lower, and her left leg weakness made that impossible. It was 1 p.m. and we were supposed to leave about 5 p.m. I immediately became tense thinking this was not going to work out after all the efforts in planning that we had done! I frantically looked up on the internet various options for garage opener repair. I needed someone who could come quickly.

I managed to find a service from Bloomington that was able to come out that afternoon. They arrived about 3 p.m. and I explained that I really needed to be able to leave using the Honda CRV at 5 p.m. I certainly needed to have them be done also by that time as I could not leave the house unattended with an unknown repairman. I helped the technician as I could to help move things along. He ended up having to replace the garage door opener and finished just in time so that I could take Jane. I do not often get headaches, but I had a splitting tension headache by the time this was done, and we were to leave. I was hoping that Tylenol would take care of this headache to be able to enjoy the evening with Jane's family.

It turned out that Sandra and Lou were able to bring Helen from the transitional care unit in a wheelchair, and Jane and I were able to make it there. We had a wonderful meal and celebration for Walt. Then afterward, we got to shovel our way out of the parking lot to get everyone back home, as it snowed something like 6-8 inches that evening. It was a day that I will never forget.

January 1, 2016

I am writing this on New Year's morning 2016. Jane just told me she hopes this will be a better year than 2015. She had the two more brain surgeries in September, restarted the Avastin the Monday before Christmas because of recurrence of her tumor (although Dr. Buckner still said it was "unclear"). Unless there is some sort of miracle that I would not be able to understand, Jane will graduate to heaven sometime this year given her cancer and our lack of knowledge to be able to treat it further.

A story in the paper yesterday said that there was a storm over the Artic Ocean and the North pole that caused the temperature there to be in the 30s- yes- the 30s- which is 50 degrees above normal!!!!!!!! Global warming is accelerating, and our global society still is moving too slowly. How do I respond to help the future of humanity better- how does everyone respond? God has given us this beautiful earth to live on- we could have many, many generations of life here. Our destiny is in our hands to much extent. Will we have the ability to love one another as our neighbor and make the sacrifices that will be necessary?

Jane would tell me to never lose hope.

On Wednesday night January 13th, when it was a difficult day and evening, Jane said "I'm going to be brave."

On Thursday morning January 14th, Jane said "We have to remember God has surprises in store for us."

On Friday morning January 22nd, she said "I had a dream where I could not have surgery because I was too sparkly." That morning she also said she had a dream where we had sex. We have not been able to do that for more than two years for a variety of reasons- concern it would trigger a urine infection and pain from atrophic vaginitis along with other reasons.

Chapter Twenty One

NOTES FROM JANE TO JEFF

Over the years, Jane would write me notes to tell me that she was thinking of me.

Sometimes she put the notes in my lunch bag when I was not looking. Sometimes she left a note on my desk. But always it was a thoughtful note, a sign of her love for me, a sign that she was thinking of me. She always had impeccable timing. She knew when I needed to have her reach out to me in that fashion.

Jeff,
I love you so much and am so proud of you!
See you soon!
Love,
Jane

Jeff— see you after the movie!
♡ Jane

This is the day
the Lord has made
for you. Rejoice &
be glad in it.
♡ Jane

I Love You
&

Know you've been
under a
lot of stress.
I hope your day
goes well
♡ Jane

I see these notes now and am reminded of her amazing love and companionship that I will never forget. I can hear her speaking these words to me as if she were here right now.

On our 25th wedding anniversary, August 2, 2000, Jane wrote the following note:

Jeff,

"These things I promise to you:
I will be faithful to you and honest with you;
I will respect, trust and care for you; I
will share my life with you; I will forgive
you as we have been forgiven; and I will
try with you to understand ourselves, the world
and God; through the best and worst of
what is to come, until death parts us."

When I look at these vows I realize
how difficult a promise they are to keep
day after day and year after year. Twenty-five
years ago I said similar words to you with
all of the naivety of a young person. Now
I realize what a big commitment this is
and how hard it is at times to be true
to these words. Even so, I make these
promises to you again, with a little more
wisdom and experience.

Here's to many more years together —

Love,
Jane

To love another
is to touch the face
of God.

Victor Hugo

Chapter Twenty Two

NEVER GIVE UP HOPE

Jane had what turned out to be the last MRI of her brain on December 15, 2015. Due to signs of probable tumor recurrence, she had restarted the chemotherapy Avastin (bevacizumab) the week before Christmas of 2015 and continued it thru March 22, 2016. But it was clear to me that she was slowly worsening. Part of that was having her left side be weaker at times. Each time she had had MRIs she would hate finding out the result.

So many times, there was uncertainty about whether there was any progression. More than once, there was a difference of opinion regarding whether there was recurrence by these highly trained and caring specialists. As a family physician, I had not been aware how difficult it was to interpret brain MRIs after treatment for cancer such as hers. If there was enough recurrence to see it on an MRI, often a person was having some type of symptoms that told you before the scan that there was a problem. Patients were sometimes fearful of going on hospice rather than continuing to treat a late-stage cancer.

But I had seen many times where it seemed that a patient not only had better quality of life, but also seemed to live longer than expected by going on hospice, or comfort care. It made sense that sometimes the complications of active treatment could actually shorten a person's life. So, in late March of

2016, I talked with Jane about the hospice option, and she agreed to have a hospice consult which took place at our home on March 29th. There had been several times that we had previously discussed this option with her physicians. But this time she decided to go on hospice and to discontinue the chemotherapy.

On May 24th, Jane said "I don't want our children and friends to remember me like this." She was referring to being paralyzed and being overweight, etc. Those two things have been the hardest for her to deal with.

Jane heard a song by Jason Mraz-

She said it had a phrase-- " It's not the end- it's just the beginning." She found it a hopeful song.

I have not been able to find that song so far.

The spring and summer were filled with the daily activities of caring for Jane. I was so blessed to have so much help. Carol Ford, one of Jane's GNO group, was able to help us every Friday in the morning, and many times brought a meal that Jane and I could eat for dinner that night. Sarah continued to stay with Jane all day on Mondays and the boys helped as they were able to do so. Our neighbors Dick and Kay Lippert were always available on a moment's notice which helped more than once for the unexpected fall, etc. Given's Jane's condition, I was simply not able to get her up all by myself if she had fallen.

On July 5th, I made an entry in my diary regarding wheelchair rides:

Tom made some nice portable ramps that we can use to get Jane outside via the front door and its step to the porch and step to the sidewalk. The first time on a Thursday, I think June 23rd, we just went two houses down the street in the evening to talk with Dick and Kay Lippert as well as Gary and Joanne Rosette. Then on Tuesday 6/28 I got her out and gave her a ride to the farmhouse on 90th street in the evening and we saw the cows and fields. Jane loved taking walks, getting outside, as well as seeing the cows at the farm that was near us.

Last Friday on July 1st, Carol Ford pushed Jane in the wheelchair, and I walked with and we went as far as the driveway for the small church at the corner of 90th and County Road #19. It was a beautiful summer day- the temperature was in the 70s and there was low humidity. Then on Saturday July 2nd, Jane and I asked if Dick and Kay wanted to walk with and we went out to the church driveway again- it was a beautiful day again.

It is nice to be able to have Jane get out of the house when her mobility is so limited. It is taking increasing effort to help her transfer from the bed to the wheelchair and to the toilet and vice versa. She is sleeping more- gradually.

I have decided to take full time leave under FMLA starting next Monday. We will see how it goes. If I use up all the FMLA, I may have to retire to continue to care for her. But then we would not have any health insurance. I think of all the people in our country that have similar challenges and know that we could have better laws regarding health care. I could continue health insurance under the COBRA act, but it would be expensive at a time that we would not have any income.

Jane had a fall in the bathroom with Hazel, one of her PCAs (personal care attendants) on the evening of June 28th- Tuesday- about 9 pm. It is harder to transfer her due to the weakness on her left side. Her left arm is almost entirely flaccid now. Her left leg continues to slowly get weaker. Jane blamed herself for the fall, she did not want Hazel to feel responsible. She did not want her to think she could not help. Hazel and I were able to get Jane back up, but it took a great deal of effort on both of our parts to do that. Jane feels bad that she is as heavy as she is, but with the steroid dose she is on- dexamethasone 4 mg bid (twice daily)- she has a strong appetite, and it makes it impossible to lose weight. Dr. Cameron did not think it was safe to lower the dose of the dexamethasone, feeling there was too much chance Jane would decline faster.

As I said earlier, Jane always loved weddings. Our good friends Kathy and John Jorgensen have three children. Their oldest child, their daughter Sandy was to be married on Labor Day weekend- on September 4th, 2016. September 4th was the day that Jane's parents were married in 1948. Sandy and her fiancé had their wedding and reception set up at an older home in St. Paul on Summit avenue- a beautiful venue. It was just that logistically for Jane it would be difficult. There were no ramps for wheelchairs, no handicapped accessible bathrooms. The wedding was to be on the lawn of the home. She had not been able to get into the car- Honda CRV- since sometime in May due to her weakness and inability even with my help to transfer from the wheelchair to the car seat or vice versa. During the summer we had only gone out of the home with her in the wheelchair for walks on the street and the path on 90th Street.

Sometime in early August I made a reservation for a transport van so that we could go to the wedding with her in the wheelchair, be at the wedding, and then return home. We found out the driver could stay there during the wedding (usually with transport they would leave after dropping you off and then come back when you were ready to go). But to get dressed, go to the bathroom, then sit in the wheelchair for the ride there, during the wedding, and even if we returned home immediately after the wedding, it seemed it would be a minimum of two hours in the wheelchair. Jane was continuing to get weaker during the month of August. I think it was in early August when she decided she wanted to write a book and asked me to start recording her thoughts.

The week before Sandy's wedding- August 28th and forward- Jane was so weak that she did not sit in the wheelchair for longer than one half hour before getting tired or having her bottom be sore even with the padding that we had. I just did not see how she was going to be able to endure being in the wheelchair long enough to go to the wedding.

We had gone to Florida in late January of 2015 when I was unsure that we should go due to all her medical issues. We had gone to San Francisco in May of 2015 with part of our family despite my reservations and all the issues of trying to figure out how to have her INRs checked (we ended up getting a machine from the clinic that we took with to do the testing). We had gone to the Pink Shell Beach resort in early January of 2016 because Jane wanted to go to Florida again- yet with her weakness, it was a challenge to have her get on and off the plane due to the transfers from the wheelchair with her left sided paralysis and overall weakness. But with getting a change in her ticket to first class in the first row both going to Florida and coming back- it did work out. Sarah and Jake were with us and that made it possible. I could not have done it alone.

But the week before Labor Day 2016, I just could not see how Jane was going to be able to go in the transport so that we could attend the wedding. That Thursday I decided to cancel the transport because they had to have notice. I told her that I had done so.

As I recall later that day, she wanted me to record some thoughts for her book. One of those thoughts was that you should never give up hope. No matter what the situation, no matter how daunting or how impossible it seemed, she said that you can always have hope that things will work out.

I felt like I had taken her hope away by canceling that transport. Her spirit so wanted to be with our friends and their daughter on that wedding day- her body simply did not cooperate. I imagine that her spirit indeed was present at that wedding.

Chapter Twenty Three

THE LAST TWO MONTHS

In August of 2016, Jane decided she wanted to write a book. I was thinking it would have been good to start a little earlier since she was becoming tired so easily. But every time that she had ideas for her book, I would write them on a notebook or type them into the computer and save those notes. Due to her fatigue, on a given day I do not know that she spent more than 10-15 minutes telling me what she wanted me to write down. Sometimes she would fall asleep briefly and then wake and tell me another idea. I have written those notes largely as she told me to give you an idea of how she was thinking at the end of her life here on earth. I also do it that way because I do not know how each of you thinks and how each of you are impacted. Jane felt that she was intended to help others through her having to deal with this illness. I ask you to remember how we never know the full impact of our thoughts and words on those that we love, as well as those that we have never met in this earthly life. I know that Jane cared for so many others during her lifetime. I hope that her thoughts somehow are helpful to some of you that read this.

August 20, 2016 morning

"I want to impart some information to people."

"I feel like if there are other people that can do books, then I can do it."

"There are some books that I feel are not that good."

She wants to write a nonfiction book.

"I want to tell people what they might have to look forward to. i.e., expecting what might happen. I want to say when you are given the diagnosis of brain cancer, be sure that you connect with your doctor. Give yourself time to process the information. There are people available with lots of helpful information.

Check into equipment that will help you, like taller toilets, hospital beds, etc. Check into friends and family that might provide meals.

Use pill boxes to keep meds straight. Get a water bottle. Search out support groups."

Jane asked a group of friends/family to be her prayer group.

Jane-" Always look on the positive side of life."

Jane-"Take one thing at a time."

Jane-"Set goals for yourself."

August 20, 2016 afternoon

"Have a reliable person set up your medication and use alarms to remind you if necessary.

Some medicines require taking with food and others not.

I take yogurt as a food when meds need food- it is easy and quick.

Everyone has different experiences with seizures.

My seizures involve jerking of my eyes and limbs.

Your doctors will instruct you on what to do to manage them.

I also have trouble urinating.

What helps me is turning on water or music to relax me.

Always have someone present with you in case a seizure would happen in the bathroom.

We have PCAs that help us.

I am unable to walk by myself to the bathroom, so I need someone to come with me."

But everyone's situation is different.

I need help getting a sponge bath and dressing each day.

******* Allow your friends to offer help with meals and prayers.

You will never know how generous people can be unless you allow them to help.

My Ipad was a tremendous help during these days.

August 22, 2016

Try to get outside often.

Get some sort of exercise as regular as you can.

You may have to buy a wig to help.

Try to find a place that is accommodating- there are shops that sell wigs that are closer to your style.

Keep looking for the right thing.

If you don't find something at first, keep trying.

Realize that the steroids may make you hungrier so you may gain weight, your face and stomach become puffier.

This all is a part of taking this medicine.

All the medicines- doses may be changed to accommodate whatever symptoms you have.

If you have trouble with INRs (a blood test to check on thinning of the blood), you'll need to get them checked often, your medication may change weekly.

"I want to be truthful, but I don't want to scare people."

August 25, 2016 Thursday

Be aware of constant challenges or changes.

The CAT scan is one of the easier tests. It is shorter to do. MRIs vary in time depending on how comfortable you are in claustrophobic situations. They can be adapted to how you feel- they are not painful. Waiting for results can be anxiety producing.

Radiation is a very precise treatment where a mask is molded to your head to keep you in exactly the right position for your treatment. This test is also not painful. Each treatment episode is fairly quick. It can cause fatigue and some loss of hair.

September 1, 2016 Thursday

Challenges like using a wheelchair, wearing Depends, not being able to wash your hair as often as you like, gaining weight, changing clothing size. These all can be very frustrating as your body image changes. You may feel like a different person.

(Jeff's thought- In a sense, you are a different person than you were before.)

Some treats that I found to be helpful are tubs of Animal Crackers from Sam's Club, baked potato chips, Gatorade, fruit, oatmeal, flavored Chex cereal (Vanilla).

Try not to concentrate on things that get you down. i.e., Try to think about good things.

Be grateful for what others have done for you. (Jeff's thought- Jane is an expert at that.)

She would send thank you notes as long as she could, then ask me to do it when she could not.

"Find something you enjoy doing."

"I listened to audio books because I can't read very well now."

"Have somebody read to you and summarize newspaper and magazine articles."

"This is very difficult during the 2016 political campaign."

"NEVER GIVE UP ON YOUR DREAMS."

"DON'T LET OTHER PEOPLE MAKE YOU GIVE UP ON YOUR DREAMS."

"SOMETHING I WAS TOLD TO DO WAS TO HELP OTHER PEOPLE."

"BE KIND TO YOUR LOVED ONES. IT IS EASY TO GET FRUSTRATED WITH EACH OTHER."

September 2, 2016 Friday

"Don't catastrophize."

"Think about today."

Don't worry about tomorrow.

(Jeff's thought- Be aware high dose steroids can aggravate anxiety.)

September 4, 2016 Sunday - She was confused in the morning and thought I was her mom. I am wondering if this is medication side effect. Could it be increasing brain pressure?

September 5, 2016 The Green Purse

I think Jane would want me to include how we used her green purse- a cloth purse with multiple pockets to hold what she needed when we went to appointments etc. There was a compartment to keep the medicines that we needed for the day. A pocket to hold a small bottle of water to be able to take her medication. A small supply of food- a granola bars or crackers if she got hungry. Kleenex, pads for the underwear for drip incontinence, etc.

We always kept Tylenol in it, (generic acetaminophen), anti-nausea med- ondansetron, Pepcid(famotidine) for her heartburn, 3 bottles of 1oz each liquid antacid for the acute heartburn. We had clonazepam for the possibility of seizures.

AT GNO get together- Jody asked Jane "How are you writing your book?"

Jane responded, "Wherever my brain takes me."

September 7, 2016 "SHARE YOUR STORIES" Jane said. She did not have any further ideas or energy that day.

September 10 Saturday
(Headache bothering her today.)
"Take Tylenol as often as I could and take Gatorade- also ondansetron."

(Jeff's thoughts)
JOG talk from Cursillo- Joy of Giving-
Jane to me exemplifies the theme of this talk- she loved to give to others- loved to remember what they liked or desired and so she let people know that they were worthy, and she cared about them.

Her thoughts- my wording-
Using powder(mycostatin) helped to control rash under breast and axilla.
Keeping clean helped to prevent trouble with the perineum.

She wanted to include "about powder and keeping clean."

September 12, 2016 - Monday- "Keep yourself dry and clean."
Some help for other people to know that they are not the only ones---

September 15, 2016- Put her dreams in the book.
    "Dream of being able to get in the car (after she couldn't).
    "Dream of walking again."

September 16, "Use a white board to list appointments/who's coming"
    (It was her idea about 1 month ago- I asked Carol Ford to get them for us and we used them the last month.)

September 17, 2016—In the morning she said, "I wish you could get next to me in bed and hug me."

"I wanted to be a volunteer at Disney World."

September 18, 2016 a.m.- "I do think that some of these books (e.g., Heaven Is For Real, Proof of Heaven) are not for me--- that when God speaks, he speaks to me."
"I feel like when the Holy Spirit talked to me, He said- "I want you to help people."

September 27, 2016-- 6 am—
I asked her "Are you ready to go to heaven?"
She said "Yes."

8:30 a.m.- "I feel like Jack. He's always thirsty."
She said this very clearly after asking for orange juice- gave her sponge soaked with OJ".   (Jack is Chris and Julie's dog- we think he was water deprived at some point in his life because whenever water is available, he will drink it until it is gone.)
    11 a.m.   When giving her the lorazepam- she said "Oskar- do you want some?" (Oskar is Sarah's dog)

3 p.m. "Can I see mom and dad?"

September 28, 2016   8:30 a.m.- "I'm not talking very good today."
September 29, 2016-   2:15 a.m.-
Jeff's thoughts- "This moment may not last but right now I am at peace.
Jane is peaceful- she has been awake a while.
She coughs and I ask her if that bothers her. She nods her head to say yes. I explained that the atropine that could reduce her secretions would make her feel very dry.
And she says "ok, ok, ok" in an annoyed tone.
The clock near the tv is ticking very softly.
The light over the kitchen desk is on- softly.
The night is peaceful.
I think God's spirit is present.
Sleep is so peaceful, so wonderful.

October 3, 2016
Jane had had no food and less than an ounce of liquid each day for at least twelve days. The medicine that she needed was all in liquid form that could be absorbed in her mouth. Her coma gradually deepened. I believe that it was simply her will to live that kept her going so long. There were several times in the last few days that I had thought it was going to be the end.

That morning a little after 9 a.m., Jane died - Chris, Tom, Sarah, and I were all with her....... Her cheeks remained rosy for such a long time after she was gone.

Chapter Twenty Four

THE JOURNEY CONTINUES

In December of 2016, I found the following poem that I had written to her some time in years past. She had it in an envelope of scrapbook items-various notes and cards that she had saved.

Jane
Long strands of her blond hair brush against me,
Her blue eyes see everything.
Her soft skin makes me know she is real.
Her warmth is the fire of my heart.
Her laughter brings joy to my soul.
Her soul is the creation of the God
I can never fully understand
But whom I thank with all my being.

Perhaps she was an angel, sent to guide me through part of my life. If I wallow in self-pity grieving her death continually, then I did not learn her message of love and hope and joy. Why do we have to endure suffering? We do not know, but in living the relationships with those we love, we are blessed beyond all comprehension. I got to experience a bit of heaven by being married to Jane.

You know that you have a wonderful marriage, a wonderful loving relationship with your wife, when you just want to be with her, you just enjoy doing about anything with her, you love "to make love" with her, but you also love to just be with her, hold her hand, touch her, snuggle with her.

When you miss someone very much, you know you were blessed by love. It is a sign your relationship was very close, very good. It means you were living and are living. It is a joy to know you have loved another like that- that it hurts so much. I would rather have loved so deeply that my heart breaks, than to never have loved like that at all.

Her spirit is not bounded by space and time. It was not when she lived here on earth and it is not now that she exists in God's realm. "I can only imagine" is a wonderful song regarding the afterlife. If you have not heard it, it is worth your time.

I love to imagine Jane being next to me, being able to hold her hand, and give her a hug. I keep pictures of her around the house because I need to see her smiling face.

For some time, I continued to pray "God, please give me the strength and the patience and the wisdom that I need to manage this day." I had begun to pray that when I was exhausted physically taking care of Jane and when I was exhausted mentally. I pray for all the caregivers of those with these tragic illnesses. I continued that prayer to handle the grief following her death.

I do not believe God causes these tragedies, but I do believe God is there to help us thru these difficult times.

I know that I need to live each day, be here for our children and grandchildren, as well as our friends and family. I will continue to try to do what I think it is that God hopes for me to do while I am still on this earthly sojourn.

But when the time comes for my life to end, I hope and pray and trust that I will be able to experience the joy of my spirit being with Jane's spirit in the company of all those that have gone before us. Each one of us has some thing or things that we are meant to learn in this earthly life. I believe that God loves each one of us so dearly, that God forgives each one of us sooooo much.

I have prayed to be able to finish this book and share Jane's life with you. I have and will continue to pray that each one of you open your eyes to the presence of God in your life and the presence of God's love and forgiveness. This is most certainly the beauty of life, the joy of life, the meaning of life.

Jane would say she was no more and no less than any other person-God's forgiveness makes us equal in God's eyes. To me she was incredibly special. To God each one of us is incredibly special. Each one of us is a miracle and blessing. That was Jane's message to all of us.

Chapter Twenty Five

FRUITS OF THE SPIRIT

"But the fruit of the Spirit is love, joy, peace, patience, kindness, goodness,
faithfulness, gentleness and self-control.
Against such things there is no law."
—Galatians 5:22-23 NIV

In all my life, I have never met any person that more fully embodied the
fruit of the Holy Spirit as described in Galatians.

Jane loved her family, friends, and the rest of the world and hoped for
the best for everyone. Part of the way that she showed her love was to observe other's comments and remember what they expressed when it came
time to buy a gift for Christmas or another holiday.

Jane's joy was in giving to others and being thoughtful of others.

Jane showed the calm presence and peace of the Spirit in so many situations, even when she was anxious.

Jane was patient with me, with our children, and with her parents in so
many situations. But being patient did not mean that she would not give me
feedback. The following is an e-mail that she sent me when she felt I needed
to correct my behavior:

Subj: 1
Date 9/19/2000
To: jnelson@healtheast.org

I really think that if you want to spend more time with the kids and have them open up to you that you need to let them know in many ways that you like them and support them. Many times, your interaction with them is more criticizing and disapproving. I don't think it was Sarah's fault that she didn't know about the game and telling her to call when she got home after 6 and the game would've already started was not the time to get after her. I am so tired of feeling like we should have done something better and taking the blame for it. You could have reminded her last weekend to call since she hadn't heard. Your disapproval of her was so evident last night. There was no reason to get so upset about this. It was unfortunate but not enough to get everybody upset. One thing I need most from you is support and approval. When you talk about the kids and homework and not wanting to pay for college unless they show they are earning it I wonder what you think of them. It is only natural the way they are behaving to all this and they are such good kids. I wish you would realize how good our life is and be thankful.

Jane was kind, always being thoughtful of others, many times in a group being thoughtful to encourage the quiet one to talk or to listen when someone else was not realizing they were being a little too self-centered.

An example of her kindness was told to me by Kathie Nordtvedt who sent a card after Jane's death - In deepest Sympathy

She wrote:

" I didn't know Jane until she helped me one day years ago.

Jane's Random Act of Kindness was while I was at St. Luke's Christmas Bazaar.

I had "froze" due to my Parkinson's, she came to the rescue! Helped me "unfreeze," drove me home, got me in my home, and arranged for my car to get home. What an angel! Due to leaving St. Luke's I did not meet her again. My loss I am sure.

So sorry to read of her struggle w/cancer & what a journey.

Thinking & praying for you & your family.

Jane simply was so often good- it was rare for her to be thinking negative thoughts of others- especially after she became ill. She focused on celebrating life. "Live like today will be one of your best days." Jane's phrase was fired into the pottery bowl that Melissa Werpy gave me after Jane's death. Throughout my relationship with Jane, I never had to wonder if she was telling me the truth. I never had to question if she might be lying- even a little bit. This honesty made our relationship so strong.

Jane was faithful in many ways. She volunteered her time so much at church and at school for our children and at Woodwinds Hospital before she became ill. She participated in Bible study and led the women's Bible study at St. Luke Lutheran for many years. She loved serving as wedding coordinator at church, helping couples begin their married life.

Jane was so often gentle. She knew how to guide me when I became too focused on the environment or politics or religion. She knew how to gently hold a newborn infant to let them know they were loved. She knew how to use her resources to let someone know that they were special.

Jane was an example of self-control. She was the eternal diplomat. If she was upset, it was rare for her to show it.

Jane was not perfect. I lived with her for over 41 years. We had our good moments and our bad moments together. But as I said, she embodied the Holy Spirit in her being more than any other person that I have had the privilege to meet. Other than the gift of Christ Jesus to forgive our sins, to me Jane was the best gift God ever gave me. And I have been given many gifts of family and friendship in my life. I am forever thankful for the time I was able to share with Jane here on this earthly journey. And I believe that her spirit is still here with me in part at the same time that her spirit is with God. I do not know how that works, but I don't have to fully understand. All things are possible with God.

Jane would not want me to focus on her.

A Devotional called the Daily Word is printed by the Unity Church. In the January 19, 2017 devotion, it is stated "The Christ Presence within me is my greatest source of inner peace." I believe that God created me, sustains me, and forgives me. Until reading some of the Unity devotional material, I had not considered the idea that God's spirit is within me. But as I say that, now I am reminded of the blessing that Pastor Joel Bexell would say at the end of the worship service at St. Luke Lutheran in Cottage Grove:

As you go on your way,
May God go with you.
May he go before you to show you the way,
Behind you to encourage you,
Beside you to befriend you,
Above you to watch over you,
And within you to give you peace.
In the name of the Father, and the Son, and
the Holy Spirit. Amen.

Jane would want me to focus on the love that God has for each and every one of us.

It is fitting for me to finish with something that Jane had written to be a part of her funeral service:

What I Have Learned From Life-- by Jane Nelson

"Live life like today will be one of your best days and not one of your worst days.

Be brave, be forgiving. Be the bigger person. Don't sweat the small stuff, it doesn't matter. You don't always have to be right; it really doesn't matter. Be loving and friendly. Always greet people with a smile and hello if nothing else. Love yourself. Go to church and you will be reminded how to live life in the way Jesus wants you to. It will keep you on the right path. You will feel good about yourself. Life is not fair but holds many good times. Always be on the lookout for them. They far outweigh the bad times. If not, relook at how you are living your life. Bad things happen. Have faith.

Not everyone is going to like you. That's just how it is. Sadness is a part of life. See the movie *Inside Out*.

Trust God. You may not like where he leads you though. God wants you to have a wonderful life. He loves you more than anyone. He loves us all the same. That is what forgiveness brings.

Keep friendships alive.

I don't want this to be too long, so I want you to celebrate not only my life but all of life, especially yours. Go home and celebrate your life."

I don't think I can ever "finish" this book because I will feel that her story is not done. The effect that Jane had on her loved ones- our children, myself, her siblings, her friends, and many others continues in this world and I trust in the next world as well.

God created a beautiful spirit when God created Jane.

She never gave up faith. She never gave up hope. She continued to always love.

"Faith, hope, and love abide, but the greatest of these is love."

Again, Jane would not want me to focus on her. I ask each of you that reads this book to remember that you are an amazing spirit- God created you that way and his love and forgiveness sustain you through all of life's trials.

Chapter Twenty Six

SURROGATE GRANDMA

Jane had wanted so much to be a grandmother. She was so thrilled when our first grandchild, Ruby Jane, was born in August of 2015 and when our grandson, Ben, was born in February 2016. She enjoyed every moment that she was able to share with them and our children and their spouses. She knew there would be more grandchildren. She was sad that she would not be able to be here in physical form to help nurture them and live life with them. I know that if there is any way possible, she will be with them in spiritual form- however and whatever that means. But since she was not going to be able to be here physically for them, she wanted someone she trusted to act as grandmother for her. She asked my sister Janet to be that surrogate grandma. So, Aunt Janet has become another grandmother to my grandchildren.

Janet is an RN who had worked years ago in a cardiac telemetry unit, had worked as the head of a student health clinic at a college in the Milwaukee area, as well as a clinic nurse. She and her husband Marc were married in Iowa, shortly after Christmas the first year that I was in practice in Cottage Grove. I remember that vividly for more than their wedding and the association with Christmas that year. That evening at their reception, I came down with influenza.

I had significant fever and chills as well as aching and cough. On the return home to Cottage Grove the following day, I was ill enough that I could not drive that 6-hour route. So, Jane who was 7 months pregnant drove the entire way. Chris was in his car seat in the back of the car, and I was in the front passenger seat. As we approached Rochester, Minnesota on U.S. highway 52, we encountered ice on a bridge. Jane was a very good driver, but the ice was so slick that the car spun around, and we slid off the road. We were going backward as we slid down the side of the highway an awfully long way. I will never forget that view. Fortunately, we did not roll over and none of us was hurt physically. We just had the anxiousness that is caused by such an episode. Seatbelts work well in that circumstance. I was able to hitchhike a short distance to get a tow for our car. Again, in those days you did not have cell phones to contact someone. I did not realize that tow trucks could have a long enough tow rope to pull out a car which was at least 75 feet down the hill off the highway. But the tow truck driver was able to attach to the axle of the car and gently pulled it back to the road. We made it the rest of the way home and then Jane came down with the influenza. Thankfully, we had neighbors that were willing to get groceries for us, and Jane's parents were able to help take care of Chris when both of us were so ill. There was no medicine like Tamiflu (oseltamivir) in those days to shorten the duration of that illness. It was less than two months later that Jane delivered Tom by C-section.

Janet and Marc have two sons, Nick and Will. At the time Jane had her brain cancer, neither were married or had any children. More importantly, Janet visited us numerous times during Jane's journey with brain cancer. Whenever she was able to visit, she was always a tremendous help. She loved to cook and made many meals for us while she was there. It was a great chance to have the children and grandchildren over for a meal that was little to no work for Jane and me. Janet would get whatever groceries were needed, help me with any chores that needed to be done, and just helped us be able to enjoy the time together.

I had continued to work about half-time during the duration of Jane's illness, and when I was not working at the clinic, there was usually something that needed to be done at home. So, whenever there was help like that, it made it easier to enjoy some time relaxing with Jane. She and I were both very thankful for the gift of Janet's help. Janet says that it made her feel good that Jane allowed her to do things for our family. The two of them so exemplified the joy of giving and receiving.

Janet says that she learned a lot from Jane about cooking. She recalls a time that Jane was laying in the hospital bed in the family room of our home and Janet was cooking a meal for us. Jane would share different tidbits about how she would make a recipe or modify it. Janet has many recipes from Jane that are on recipe cards written by Jane for her. Seeing Jane's handwriting on those recipe cards is one way that Jane remains present for her. Janet notes that Jane was so very tactful and kind when giving her any input on cooking or other matters.

In December of 2014, Jane was recovering from her second brain surgery and had the severe left sided arm and leg weakness. Janet came to visit before Christmas. She wrapped nearly all the Christmas gifts for the family since Jane was not able to do that. She helped us celebrate Jane's birthday on the 16th of that month. She participated in our annual making of lefse to keep up the tradition that Jane's parents- Walt and Helen- had taught us. Janet says that Jane never made her feel bad. My sister says that Jane made you feel good about what you brought to the table in life.

Jane loved going to Sanibel Island in Florida and shelling on the beaches there. Janet says that encouraged her and Marc to start going there for a winter vacation. She recalls a visit to our home where she and Jane made a craft using various items including shells from Sanibel. Janet and Marc continue to go there yearly for some warmth and sun in the middle of our winters.

Also, Jane and Janet had shared some special moments together. One of those times was at Grand View Lodge on the weekend in 2011 that Sarah and Jake were married. After the rehearsal dinner was done, the family members had scattered, and many were getting ready for sleep for the busy day ahead. Rumor has it that two women whose names start with J found that skinny-dipping in Gull Lake was a good way to relax that evening.

Chapter Twenty Seven

POEM

I am your mother.
I wonder what your future holds.
I hear your laughter, your complaints, your desires, your fears.
I see you grow with each passing day.
I want so much for you to be happy and healthy.
I am your mother.

I pretend sometimes that you are still small.
I feel your warmth and smell your scent.
I touch your hair, your face, your soft skin.
I worry that harm may come to you.
I cry when you're hurting or unhappy.
I am your mother.

I understand more than you think.
I say more than I should at times.
I dream that life will be good to you.
I try to do what is right for you.
I hope you keep God in your heart.
I am your loving mother.

The poem was written by Jane at one of the women's retreats that St. Luke Lutheran church sponsored according to Irene Detviler, a friend of ours from church. One time that Irene visited us in August of 2015, she had brought a copy and asked if Jane remembered writing it. Jane had never mentioned it to me before that time. To me it is an example of the love that she had for our children and all people, and an example of her beautiful creativity.

Chapter Twenty Eight

POSTSCRIPT

I had never written a personal type of letter to a president, but in the summer of 2016, I decided to send the following letter on July 19th:

Dear President and Mrs. Obama,

First, we would like to thank you for being such role models as parents, leaders, and members of our society. We will miss you when your terms as President and First Lady are finished. We thank you for your service to our country at a time that has been so difficult in so many ways. We hope and trust that you will continue to serve our country in other ways after this year.

Despite our current personal tragedy, we feel that we have been blessed in so many ways by this country of ours. We hope for our children and grandchildren that they will have the opportunities that we have been blessed with.

Jane and I met at college and were married almost 41 years ago. Jane supported me in medical school, and together we raised our three children, all of whom are married, and in the last year we have been blessed with two grandchildren.

In early 2014, at age 60 Jane was the picture of health- she never smoked, got regular walking exercise, ate healthy and looked like she would live into her 90s as many in her family have. Then one day she fell unwitnessed and was diagnosed with an aggressive type of brain cancer, has undergone four brain surgeries, radiation therapy, chemotherapy, suffered seizures, blood clots, pulmonary emboli, fractures of her arm, and later of her clavicle and several ribs, and has been paralyzed on the left side since her second surgery in December of 2014. She had experimental surgery at the Mayo Clinic last year and now has been on hospice since early April. Her faith hope and love has inspired all of us to continue to believe in the future no matter what events transpire.

When she was diagnosed, one of her goals was to be present at our son Tom's wedding in June of 2014 to his wife Darcy. In February, the next year when they announced Darcy was pregnant, one of her goals was to be alive when Ruby Jane was born in August of 2015. When our son Chris and his wife Julie announced their pregnancy that summer of 2015, her goal was to be alive when our grandson Ben was born in February of 2016. Now her goal is to be at Ruby's first birthday. She has lived each day as the gift that it is and made the most of a difficult situation.

We believe that each one of us is called by our creator to make a contribution to life and our society during our time here on earth. We are concerned regarding our society's treatment of this world that we all need to live in- the water, the air, the land that we so easily take for granted. We thank you for your efforts to improve our care of this environment that we all need. We will try to continue to do our part thru energy conservation, recycling, contributing to organizations such as the Nature Conservancy, the World Wildlife Fund, etc.

We happen to be Christians in our faith, but we embrace the diversity of our culture and all the different faiths that exist in our society. We all have so much to learn from each other. Even within each faith, there are so many variations in belief. We do believe that God tries to reach out to all of us in so many different ways. We do believe that God's main theme for all of us is the love and mercy that God has for each of us, and that God expects each of us to have that same love and mercy for each other.

Once again, we send our thanks for the inspiration that you and your family have provided to us as well as many other citizens of our country. God bless you and your family in the coming years.

Sincerely yours,

Jeff and Jane Nelson and family

In November of 2016, about a month after Jane had died, we received this response to our letter.

THE WHITE HOUSE

WASHINGTON

November 2, 2016

Mrs. Jane Nelson
Cottage Grove, Minnesota

Dear Jane:

During this tremendously difficult time, Michelle and I want you to know we are thinking of you.

The courage and character you are demonstrating reflect the power of the human spirit. I hope you draw strength from the love and support of those around you, and from the beliefs you carry in your heart.

Please know you and your family will remain in my thoughts.

Sincerely,

9 781946 195890